Imaginative ways with RICE & PULSES

In our health-conscious world, rice, grains and beans have been elevated from humble peasant food — until recently thought of as fattening and stodgy — to being fashionable and good for you. This new status has inspired recipes and ideas that turn these foods into gourmet dishes, and has created an awareness of different cuisines as we look for new ways in which to use them.
In this book you will find a host of wonderful dishes, including traditional risottos, gourmet lentil burgers, imaginative salads and much more.

CONTENTS

Starters 2
Main Meals 10
Quick Meals 28
Risottos 38
Vegetarian 44
Salads 50
Side Dishes 58
Techniques 64
Ingredients 74
Index 79

THE PANTRY SHELF
Unless otherwise stated, the following ingredients used in this book are:
Cream   Double, suitable for whipping
Flour   White flour, plain or standard
Sugar   White sugar

WHAT'S IN A TABLESPOON?
NEW ZEALAND
1 tablespoon =
15 mL OR 3 teaspoons
UNITED KINGDOM
1 tablespoon =
15 mL OR 3 teaspoons
AUSTRALIA
1 tablespoon =
20 mL OR 4 teaspoons
The recipes in this book were tested in Australia where a 20 mL tablespoon is standard. All measures are level.

The tablespoon in the New Zealand and United Kingdom sets of measuring spoons is 15 mL. In many recipes this difference will not matter. For recipes using baking powder, gelatine, bicarbonate of soda, small quantities of flour and cornflour, simply add another teaspoon for each tablespoon specified.

RECIPE COLLECTION

STARTERS

Many of the recipes in this chapter will also stand on their own as light meals or snacks. Starting a meal with a dish based on rice, grains or beans is an economical way to fill hungry teenagers.

Chilli Rice Balls

Mushroom and Barley Soup

Rice-filled Tomatoes

Dolmades

Lentil Wontons

Hearty Bean Soup

Red Bean Dip

Chilli Rice Balls

CHILLI RICE BALLS

STARTERS

1 tablespoon olive oil
1 onion, finely chopped
1 1/2 cups/330 g/10 1/2 oz rice
1/2 teaspoon ground turmeric
3 cups/750 mL/1 1/4 pt chicken stock
1/2 teaspoon chilli powder
freshly ground black pepper
3 spring onions, finely chopped
15 g/1/2 oz butter
3 tablespoons grated tasty cheese
(mature Cheddar)
2 eggs, lightly beaten
125 g/4 oz mozzarella cheese, cut into 16 cubes
3/4 cup/90 g/3 oz dried breadcrumbs
oil for deep-frying

1 Heat olive oil in a frying pan, add onion and cook for 2-3 minutes or until soft. Stir in rice and turmeric and cook, stirring, for 1-2 minutes longer or until rice is coated with oil.

2 Pour 3/4 cup/185 mL/6 fl oz stock into frying pan and bring to the boil. Cook, stirring frequently, until liquid has almost evaporated. Add chilli powder, black pepper to taste and remaining stock and simmer for 10-15 minutes or until liquid has been absorbed and rice is tender. Remove pan from heat and stir in spring onions, butter and tasty cheese (mature Cheddar).

3 Fold eggs into rice mixture, taking care not to mash the grains. Divide rice mixture into sixteen equal portions. Take a cheese cube and, using wet hands, mould one portion of rice around a cheese cube, to form a ball. Repeat with remaining rice and cheese.

4 Roll balls in breadcrumbs, place on a plate lined with plastic food wrap and refrigerate for 30 minutes. Heat oil in a deep saucepan until a cube of bread dropped in browns in 50 seconds. Cook 4-5 rice balls at a time for 5 minutes, or until golden. Using a slotted spoon, remove balls and drain on absorbent kitchen paper. Serve immediately.

Makes 16

Great to serve as a pre-dinner nibble or as a starter, these rice balls are also delicious served with a homemade tomato sauce and green salad as a light meal.

'Raw rice cooks up to about three times its volume. If a recipe calls for 1/2 cup/100 g/3 1/2 oz rice, cooked, you would expect to have about 1 1/2 cups/330 g/10 1/2 oz of cooked rice.'

RECIPE COLLECTION

Mushroom and Barley Soup

Mushroom and Barley Soup

One of the simplest soups you will ever make. Use either pot or pearl (scotch) barley for this recipe. Pearl barley is the refined grain, so it takes less time to cook than pot barley.

500 g/1 lb button mushrooms, sliced
1 tomato, chopped
2 carrots, chopped
1 onion, chopped
2 stalks celery, chopped
2 tablespoons chopped fresh parsley
1/2 cup/100 g/3 1/2 oz barley
6 cups/1.5 litres/2 1/2 pt water
freshly ground black pepper

Place mushrooms, tomato, carrots, onion, celery, parsley, barley and water in a large saucepan and bring to the boil. Reduce heat, cover and simmer for 1 hour or until barley is tender. Season to taste with black pepper.

Serves 4

Rice-filled Tomatoes

STARTERS

4 tomatoes
2 tablespoons vegetable oil
1 onion, finely chopped
1/3 cup/75 g/2 1/2 oz rice, cooked
1/2 green pepper, chopped
3 canned tomatoes, drained and chopped
2 tablespoons sour cream
freshly ground black pepper

CREAMY LEEK SAUCE
15 g/1/2 oz butter
1 leek, white part only, sliced
1/4 cup/60 mL/2 fl oz dry white wine
3/4 cup/185 mL/6 fl oz cream (double)

1 Cut tops from tomatoes and, using a teaspoon, scoop out centre and discard.

2 Heat oil in a large frying pan, add onion, rice, green pepper and canned tomatoes and cook, stirring, for 3 minutes. Stir in sour cream and black pepper to taste. Divide rice mixture between tomatoes. Place tomatoes in a lightly greased baking dish and cook for 10 minutes.

3 To make sauce, melt butter in a saucepan, add leek and cook for 1 minute. Stir in wine and cream and cook over a high heat for 5 minutes or until mixture is reduced by half. Serve with tomatoes.

Serves 4

Oven temperature
180°C, 350°F, Gas 4

Rice is one of the oldest cultivated crops. The first reliable mention of rice comes from China, where it is recorded that in about 2800 BC the Chinese Emperor Shen established a rice-planting ceremony.

Rice-filled Tomatoes

RECIPE COLLECTION

DOLMADES

375 g/12 oz packaged vine leaves, rinsed
2 cups/500 mL/16 fl oz vegetable or chicken stock

RICE AND LENTIL FILLING
60 g/2 oz brown rice, cooked
60 g/2 oz red lentils, cooked
2 spring onions, chopped
1 small tomato, peeled and chopped
2 tablespoons chopped toasted pine nuts
1/2 teaspoon finely grated lemon rind
1 tablespoon lemon juice
2 teaspoons chopped fresh basil
1 clove garlic, crushed
2 teaspoons olive oil

1 Place vine leaves in a saucepan, cover with water and set aside for 5 minutes. Bring to the boil, then drain and cool.

2 To make filling, place rice, lentils, spring onions, tomato, pine nuts, lemon rind, lemon juice, basil, garlic and oil in a bowl and mix well to combine. Divide filling between twenty vine leaves and roll up leaves tightly to form neat parcels.

3 Place rolls close together in a large heavy-based frying pan and cover with remaining vine leaves. Place a plate over rolls to prevent them from unrolling during cooking. Add stock to cover rolls. Cover pan, bring to the boil, then reduce heat and simmer for 45 minutes.

Makes 20

Through the ages rice has been such an important food that in some languages the word for rice and food is the same. So in some countries asking someone if they have had rice means 'Have you eaten?'.

LENTIL WONTONS

15 g/1/2 oz dried mushrooms
boiling water
100 g/3 1/2 oz spinach, finely chopped
1 tablespoon dry sherry
60 g/2 oz cabbage, finely chopped
2 teaspoons soy sauce
1/2 teaspoon sesame oil
2 teaspoons grated fresh ginger
4 spring onions, finely chopped
75 g/2 1/2 oz red lentils, cooked
40 prepared wonton wrappers
1 egg, beaten with 3 tablespoons water
vegetable oil for deep-frying

CORIANDER SAUCE
1 tablespoon white vinegar
1/2 cup/125 mL/4 fl oz water
1 teaspoon soy sauce
3 tablespoons honey
1/2 teaspoon sesame oil
1/2 teaspoon grated fresh ginger
1/2 teaspoon sweet chilli sauce
2 teaspoons chopped fresh coriander

1 Place mushrooms in a bowl and cover with boiling water. Set aside to soak for 20 minutes. Drain, remove stalks, if necessary, and finely chop mushrooms.

2 Place mushrooms, spinach, sherry, cabbage, soy sauce, sesame oil, ginger, spring onions and lentils in a bowl and mix to combine. Place a teaspoon of lentil mixture on each wonton wrapper. Brush edges with egg mixture and gather up wrapper, pressing edges firmly together.

3 To make sauce, place vinegar, water, soy sauce, honey, sesame oil, ginger, chilli sauce and coriander in a small saucepan and cook over a low heat for 4-5 minutes.

4 Heat oil in a deep saucepan and cook wontons for 5 minutes or until golden and crisp. Serve with sauce for dipping.

Makes 40

Lentils range in colour from green to brown. The red lentil is the oldest known variety and continues to be the one most used. Red lentils have a subtle spicy flavour and are purchased skinned and split. Brown lentils are red lentils with the outer skins still attached.

Dolmades, Lentil Wontons

STARTERS

7

RECIPE COLLECTION

Hearty Bean Soup

Hearty Bean Soup

185 g/6 oz dried haricot beans
1 tablespoon oil
2 onions, chopped
2 cloves garlic, crushed
2 carrots, sliced
2 stalks celery, sliced
2 potatoes, chopped
440 g/14 oz canned tomatoes, undrained and mashed
6 cups/1.5 litres/2 1/2 pt water
2 tablespoons chopped fresh parsley
freshly ground black pepper

1 Place beans in a large bowl, cover with water and set aside to soak overnight.

2 Drain beans, place in a large saucepan with enough water to cover and bring to the boil. Boil for 10 minutes, reduce heat and simmer for 1 hour or until beans are soft. Drain and reserve 2 cups/500 mL/ 16 fl oz of cooking water. Place reserved cooking water and half the beans in a food processor or blender and process until smooth.

3 Heat oil in a large saucepan, add onions and garlic and cook, stirring, for 4-5 minutes or until onions are soft. Add carrots, celery, potatoes, tomatoes, water, beans and bean purée and bring to the boil. Reduce heat and simmer for 20 minutes or until vegetables are tender. Stir in parsley and season to taste with black pepper.

Serves 4

Did you know the Egyptians left dried beans in the pyramids of the Pharaohs? They believed the beans were helpful in conveying the soul to heaven.

8

Red Bean Dip

STARTERS

2 tablespoons vegetable oil
1 clove garlic, crushed
1 onion, chopped
1 fresh green chilli, seeded and finely chopped
1 teaspoon chilli powder
440 g/14 oz canned red kidney beans, drained and liquid reserved
60 g/2 oz grated tasty cheese (mature Cheddar)
tortilla chips

1 Heat oil in a large frying pan, add garlic, onion, chilli and chilli powder and cook over a medium heat, stirring, for 4 minutes or until onion is soft.

2 Place all but 3 tablespoons beans in a food processor or blender and process until smooth. Add bean purée and 2 tablespoons reserved liquid to pan and mix well to combine.

3 Stir in cheese and reserved beans and cook, stirring constantly, for 2-3 minutes or until cheese melts. Serve dip warm with tortilla chips.

Serves 6

This recipe can also be made using dried red kidney beans but they will need to be soaked and cooked first. After soaking the water should be discarded and fresh water added for cooking. When cooking red kidney beans they must be boiled for 10 minutes first. This removes haemagglutinins or toxins in the beans that cause nausea, vomiting and diarrhoea. The heat is then reduced to a simmer and the beans are cooked for $1^{1}/_{4}$-$1^{1}/_{2}$ hours or until tender.

Red Bean Dip

RECIPE COLLECTION

Main Meals

Salmon Rice Loaf

Cabbage Rolls

Brown Rice and Beef Pie

Baked Cheese Custard

Rice-filled Eggplant

Easy Paella

Lima Bean Hotpot

Sausage-filled Peppers

Chickpea Fritters

Rice Terrine

Black Bean Hotpot

Barley Casserole

Poussin with Rice Stuffing

Rainbow Risotto

Vegetable and Rice Pie

Vegetable Chilli

Rice with Cheese and Herbs

Polenta and Salami Bake

Rice, beans and grains can form the basis of many satisfying main course dishes. Combine them with fish or meat to extend these foods or with vegetables for a tasty vegetarian meal – add some herbs and spices and you have a wonderful balance of flavours, textures and nutrients.

Salmon Rice Loaf

Salmon Rice Loaf

MAIN MEALS

10 spinach leaves, stalks removed
440 g/14 oz canned salmon, drained and flaked
3 eggs, beaten
3 tablespoons sour cream or natural yogurt
2 tablespoons mayonnaise
1 tablespoon lemon juice
2 tablespoons rice, cooked
2 tablespoons grated Parmesan cheese
freshly ground black pepper

1 Boil, steam or microwave spinach leaves until tender.

2 Line the base and sides of a greased ovenproof 11 x 21 cm/4^1/$_2$ x 8^1/$_2$ in loaf tin with half the spinach leaves, allowing some of the leaves to hang over the sides of the pan.

3 Squeeze excess moisture from the remaining leaves and chop. Place chopped leaves, salmon, eggs, sour cream or yogurt, mayonnaise, lemon juice, rice, Parmesan cheese and black pepper to taste in a bowl and mix to combine.

4 Spoon salmon mixture into prepared loaf tin and fold overhanging leaves over top of mixture. Cover with aluminium foil and bake for 45 minutes or until the filling is firm. Allow the loaf to stand for 10 minutes before turning out and serving.

Serves 4

Oven temperature
200 C, 400 F, Gas 6

This loaf cooks quickly in the microwave. Remember to use a microwave-safe dish. Preparation of the loaf is the same, but cover the dish with microwave-safe plastic food wrap, then cook on HIGH (100%) for 13 minutes. Stand for 5 minutes before turning out and serving.
You will find that 2 tablespoons of uncooked rice as used in this recipe will cook up to about 6 tablespoons of cooked rice. So if you have leftover rice it could be used to make this delicious loaf.

Cabbage Rolls

8 large cabbage leaves
1 cup/250 mL/8 fl oz tomato purée
^{1}/$_2$ cup/125 mL/4 fl oz orange juice

RICE FILLING
^{1}/$_3$ cup/75 g/2^1/$_2$ oz rice, cooked
60 g/2 oz chopped peanuts
4 spring onions, chopped
2 cloves garlic, crushed
1 egg, lightly beaten
60 g/2 oz grated tasty cheese (mature Cheddar)
2 fresh red chillies, seeded and chopped
1 teaspoon dried marjoram leaves
freshly ground black pepper

1 Trim thick stalks from cabbages leaves. Boil, steam or microwave leaves until wilted. Drain and set aside.

2 To make filling, place rice, peanuts, spring onions, garlic, egg, cheese, chillies, marjoram and black pepper to taste in a bowl and mix to combine. Divide filling between leaves, fold in the sides and roll up to form neat parcels. Place parcels side by side in a shallow ovenproof dish.

3 Place tomato purée and orange juice in a small bowl and whisk to combine. Pour tomato mixture over rolls, cover and bake for 30 minutes.

Serves 4

Oven temperature
180 C, 350 F, Gas 4

Uncooked rice will keep for a year or more if stored in an airtight container in a cool, dry place.

RECIPE COLLECTION

Brown Rice and Beef Pie

Oven temperature
180°C, 350°F, Gas 4

2 large eggplant (aubergines), cut into 5 mm/¼ in slices
½ cup/125 mL/4 fl oz olive oil
1 onion, chopped
2 cloves garlic, crushed
500 g/1 lb minced lean beef
440 g/14 oz canned tomatoes, undrained and mashed
1 tablespoon finely chopped fresh oregano or 1 teaspoon dried oregano
2 tablespoons tomato paste (purée)
freshly ground black pepper
1 cup/220 g/7 oz brown rice, cooked
250 g/8 oz fresh or frozen peas, cooked
90 g/3 oz grated tasty cheese (mature Cheddar)
3 tablespoons grated Parmesan cheese
4 tablespoons dried breadcrumbs

1   Brush eggplant (aubergines) with oil. Heat half the remaining oil in a large frying pan. Place a single layer of eggplant (aubergines) in pan and cook for 4-5 minutes each side or until golden. Remove and drain on absorbent kitchen paper. Repeat with remaining eggplant (aubergines).

2   Heat remaining oil in pan, add onion and garlic and cook for 2-3 minutes or until onion is soft. Add meat and cook, stirring occasionally, for 6-8 minutes or until meat browns.

3   Stir tomatoes, oregano, tomato paste (purée) and black pepper to taste into meat mixture, bring to simmering and simmer for 8-10 minutes or until mixture reduces and thickens. Remove pan from heat and stir in rice, peas, tasty cheese (mature Cheddar) and Parmesan cheese.

4   Sprinkle half the breadcrumbs over the base and sides of a well-greased, deep 23 cm/9 in round cake tin. Place a layer of overlapping eggplant (aubergine) slices over base and sides of tin. Spoon meat mixture into tin and pack down well using the back of a spoon.

5   Overlap remaining eggplant (aubergine) slices on top of meat mixture and sprinkle with remaining breadcrumbs. Bake for 25-30 minutes or until golden brown. Allow to stand for 5 minutes before turning out and serving.

Serves 6

Brown rice is unrefined rice and so has a higher fibre content than white rice. It also takes longer to cook and absorbs more liquid during cooking.
A more recent product available in Western countries is quick-cooking brown rice (parboiled rice). The processing of this rice involves soaking the rice, then draining and boiling or steaming it to gelatinise the starch. The rice is then cooled and dried. The end product is a light yellow-coloured rice that cooks in about the same time as white rice.

Brown Rice and Beef Pie, Baked Cheese Custard

BAKED CHEESE CUSTARD

MAIN MEALS

30 g/1 oz butter
2 leeks, washed and sliced
3 rashers bacon, chopped
1/2 red pepper, finely chopped
1/4 cup/60 g/2 oz short grain rice, cooked
1 1/2 cups/375 mL/12 fl oz milk
2 eggs, lightly beaten
1/2 teaspoon dry mustard
1 teaspoon Worcestershire sauce
1 tablespoon mayonnaise
125 g/4 oz grated tasty cheese (mature Cheddar)
2 tablespoons finely chopped fresh parsley
1 teaspoon ground paprika

Serves 4

1 Melt butter in a frying pan, add leeks, bacon and red pepper and cook, stirring, for 4-5 minutes or until leeks are soft and bacon browns. Remove pan from heat and stir in rice. Transfer rice mixture to a deep-sided ovenproof dish.

2 Place milk in a saucepan and bring almost to the boil. Remove pan from heat and whisk in eggs, mustard, Worcestershire sauce, mayonnaise, cheese and parsley. Pour milk mixture over rice mixture and sprinkle lightly with paprika.

3 Place ovenproof dish in a baking dish with enough boiling water to come halfway up the sides of the ovenproof dish and bake for 25-30 minutes or until custard is firm.

Oven temperature
180°C, 350°F, Gas 4

For a complete meal, serve this delicious savoury custard with crusty wholemeal rolls and a tossed green salad or a steamed green vegetable such as broccoli or zucchini (courgettes).

RECIPE COLLECTION

Right: Easy Paella
Below: Rice-filled Eggplant

Rice-filled Eggplant

Oven temperature
180°C, 350°F, Gas 4

The filling used in this recipe is also delicious used to fill other vegetables such as red or green peppers, zucchini (courgettes), marrow or pumpkin. For a vegetarian version of this recipe, omit the bacon.

2 eggplant (aubergines)
salt

RICE AND CHEESE FILLING
2 tablespoons olive oil
1 onion, chopped
1 clove garlic, crushed
2 rashers bacon, chopped
3 canned tomatoes, drained and chopped
1 teaspoon chopped fresh thyme
or $^1/_2$ teaspoon dried thyme
1 egg
$^1/_2$ cup/60 g/2 oz dried breadcrumbs
$^1/_3$ cup/75 g/$2^1/_2$ oz rice, cooked
60 g/2 oz grated Parmesan cheese

1 Cut eggplant (aubergines) in half lengthwise and scoop out the centre leaving a 2 cm/$^3/_4$ in thick shell. Sprinkle with salt, place upside down on absorbent kitchen paper and set aside for 15 minutes.

2 Rinse eggplant (aubergines) and pat dry with absorbent kitchen paper.

3 To make filling, place oil, onion, garlic, bacon, tomatoes, thyme, egg, breadcrumbs, rice and Parmesan cheese in a bowl and mix to combine. Divide mixture between eggplant (aubergine) shells, place in a lightly greased baking dish and bake for 30 minutes.

Serves 4

Easy Paella

MAIN MEALS

30 g/1 oz butter
1 onion, chopped
$2/3$ cup/140 g/$4^{1}/_{2}$ oz brown rice
2 cups/500 mL/16 fl oz chicken stock
250 g/8 oz cooked chicken, chopped
250 g/8 oz ham, chopped
250 g/8 oz cooked prawns, shelled, deveined and chopped
2 tablespoons lemon juice
freshly ground black pepper
2 tablespoons chopped fresh parsley

1 Heat butter in a large frying pan, add onion and cook for 5 minutes or until soft.

2 Add rice and cook, stirring, for 2 minutes. Stir in stock and bring to the boil. Reduce heat, cover and simmer for 40 minutes or until rice is tender.

3 Stir in chicken, ham, prawns, lemon juice and black pepper to taste and cook for 4-5 minutes longer. Just prior to serving, sprinkle with parsley.

Serves 6

Paella is a wonderful one-dish meal. Traditionally made with short grain rice you can in fact use any type of rice that you wish. In this version brown rice has been used, but you might like to try a mixture of brown, white and wild rice for something a little different.

15

RECIPE COLLECTION

Lima Bean Hotpot

Oven temperature
180 C, 350 F, Gas 4

250 g/8 oz dried lima or butter beans
2 tablespoons oil
2 onions, chopped
1 green pepper, chopped
4 tomatoes, chopped
1/2 cup/125 mL/4 fl oz vegetable stock or water
1 tablespoon chopped fresh oregano or 1 teaspoon dried oregano
2 teaspoons chilli sauce
freshly ground black pepper
125 g/4 oz grated tasty cheese (mature Cheddar)

1 Place beans in a large bowl, cover with water and set aside to soak overnight. Drain beans, place in a saucepan with enough water to cover and bring to the boil. Boil for 10 minutes, then reduce heat and simmer for 1 hour or until beans are tender. Drain and set aside.

2 Heat oil in a saucepan, add onions and green pepper and cook, stirring occasionally, for 4-5 minutes or until vegetables are soft. Add tomatoes, stock or water, oregano and chilli sauce and bring to the boil. Reduce heat and simmer, uncovered, for 15 minutes or until sauce reduces and thickens. Stir in beans and black pepper to taste.

3 Transfer bean mixture to an ovenproof dish, sprinkle with cheese and bake for 20 minutes.

Serves 4

In most recipes that call for dried beans you can in fact use canned beans if you wish. As canned beans are already cooked, the preparation time of a dish is considerably reduced.

Left: Lima Bean Hotpot
Below: Sausage-filled Peppers

MAIN MEALS

SAUSAGE-FILLED PEPPERS

4 red peppers

SAUSAGE FILLING
1 tablespoon vegetable oil
1 onion, chopped
3 cloves garlic, crushed
4 thin beef sausages, cooked and chopped
2 teaspoons ground coriander
315 g/10 oz canned tomatoes, drained and mashed
2 teaspoons tomato paste (purée)
2 teaspoons ground cumin
440 g/14 oz canned red kidney beans, drained
1 cup/250 mL/8 fl oz cream (double)
1/3 cup/75 g/2 1/2 oz rice, cooked

1 Cut tops from red peppers and remove seeds and membranes. Set peppers aside.

2 To make filling, heat oil in a large frying pan, add onion and garlic and cook for 4-5 minutes or until onion is soft.

3 Add sausages, coriander, tomatoes, tomato paste (purée), cumin, beans and cream to pan and cook over a high heat, stirring occasionally, for 20 minutes or until mixture reduces and thickens.

4 Stir rice into tomato mixture and spoon filling into red pepper shells. Place filled red peppers in a greased baking dish and bake for 25 minutes.

Serves 4

Oven temperature
180 C, 350 F, Gas 4

When peppers are unavailable or very expensive why not have the filling without the peppers? It makes a delicious and economical meal. Simply place the filling mixture in a lightly greased ovenproof dish and bake for 15-20 minutes.

RECIPE COLLECTION

CHICKPEA FRITTERS

155 g/5 oz chickpeas
2 tablespoons chopped fresh parsley
4 spring onions, chopped
1/4 cup/60 mL/2 fl oz lime
or lemon juice
1 egg
1 tablespoon flour
1 teaspoon ground cumin
1 tablespoon chopped fresh coriander
3/4 cup/90 g/3 oz dried breadcrumbs
1/4 cup/60 mL/2 fl oz vegetable oil

YOGURT SAUCE
1 cup/200 g/6 1/2 oz natural yogurt
1 clove garlic, crushed
1 tablespoon lime or lemon juice
1 teaspoon snipped fresh chives
freshly ground black pepper

1 Place chickpeas in a large bowl, cover with water and set aside to soak overnight. Drain chickpeas, place in a saucepan with enough water to cover and bring to the boil. Boil for 10 minutes then reduce heat and simmer for 1 hour or until tender. Drain.

2 Place chickpeas, parsley, spring onions, lime or lemon juice, egg, flour, cumin and coriander in a food processor and process until smooth.

3 Roll a tablespoon of chickpea mixture into a ball, then roll in breadcrumbs and flatten to form a pattie. Place on a plate lined with plastic food wrap. Repeat with remaining chickpea mixture and breadcrumbs. Cover and refrigerate patties for 30 minutes or until ready to cook.

4 Heat oil in a large frying pan and cook patties over a medium heat for 3 minutes each side or until golden. Drain on absorbent kitchen paper.

5 To make sauce, place yogurt, garlic, lime or lemon juice, chives and black pepper to taste in a bowl and mix to combine. Serve with patties.

Serves 4

The cooking time for chickpeas can vary depending on their quality, age and place of origin.

'Chickpeas are also known as garbanzo beans. They have a delicious rich nutty flavour and are popular in Middle Eastern cuisine.'

Rice Terrine, Chickpea Fritters

RICE TERRINE

MAIN MEALS

15 g/½ oz butter
1 onion, chopped
1¼ cups/280 g/9 oz rice, cooked
1 cup/250 mL/8 fl oz milk
3 eggs
1 teaspoon chilli paste (sambal oelek)
3 tablespoons grated Parmesan cheese
2 tablespoons chopped fresh parsley
freshly ground black pepper
440 g/14 oz canned pimentos, drained

1 Melt butter in a frying pan, add onion and cook for 4-5 minutes or until soft. Remove pan from heat and set aside.

2 Place rice, milk, eggs, chilli paste (sambal oelek), Parmesan cheese, parsley, black pepper to taste and cooked onions in a bowl and mix to combine.

3 Spoon one-third of the rice mixture into a greased 11 x 21 cm/4½ x 8½ in loaf tin and top with half the pimentos. Repeat layers, ending with a layer of rice, and bake for 35-40 minutes. Allow to stand for 10 minutes before turning out and serving.

Serves 8

Oven temperature
180°C, 350°F, Gas 4

This terrine is delicious served hot, warm or cold and leftovers are always a welcome find in a packed lunch.

ST. PAUL'S R.C. SCHOOL

Above: Black Bean Hotpot
Right: Barley Casserole

Black Bean Hotpot

250 g/8 oz dried black-eyed beans
1 stalk celery, chopped
1 onion, chopped
1 bay leaf
8 spicy sausages
3 tablespoons red wine vinegar
3 tablespoons tomato purée
1 red onion, chopped
1 red pepper, chopped
freshly ground black pepper

1 Place beans in a large bowl, cover with water and set aside to soak overnight. Drain beans. Place beans, celery, onion and bay leaf in a saucepan with enough water to cover and bring to the boil. Boil for 10 minutes then reduce heat and simmer for 1 hour or until beans are tender. Drain beans, reserving $^3/4$ cup/ 185 mL/6 fl oz of cooking liquid, and discard remaining liquid and vegetables.

2 Cook sausages under a preheated grill for 5-6 minutes each side or until cooked. Slice sausages diagonally.

3 Heat reserved cooking liquid in a large frying pan, add red wine vinegar, tomato purée, red onion, red pepper, beans and black pepper to taste and simmer for 20-25 minutes or until liquid is reduced by half. Add sausages and cook for 5 minutes longer.

Serves 6

Legumes are dried beans, peas and lentils. In Western countries they are frequently eaten as canned baked beans, but form an important part of the diet of many cultures. They are an excellent source of protein, iron and fibre and are inexpensive.

Barley Casserole

MAIN MEALS

1 cup/200 g/6 1/2 oz barley
2 tablespoons vegetable oil
440 g/14 oz canned tomatoes, undrained and mashed
1/4 cup/60 mL/2 fl oz dry white wine
3 tablespoons tomato paste (purée)
1 large onion, chopped
12 stuffed green olives, halved

1 Place barley in a large bowl, cover with water and set aside to soak for 2 hours. Drain well and set aside.

2 Heat oil in a large frying pan, add barley and cook over a medium heat, stirring constantly, for 10 minutes.

3 Add tomatoes, wine and tomato paste (purée) to pan, bring to simmering and simmer for 20 minutes. Add onion and cook for 5 minutes longer. Stir in olives and serve immediately.

Serves 8

Recent studies have shown that barley foods can lower cholesterol. Beta-glucan is thought to be the ingredient responsible for this. Beta-glucan is a type of fibre which binds with cholesterol and helps with its removal from the body. It is also found in oats, but not in wheat.

RECIPE COLLECTION

Oven temperature
180°C, 350°F, Gas 4

Poussins are young chickens reared for eating that weigh approximately 375-410 g/ 12-13 oz.

POUSSIN WITH RICE STUFFING

4 x 375-410 g/12-13 oz poussins, cleaned
125 g/4 oz butter, softened
1 clove garlic, crushed
2 tablespoons snipped fresh chives
2 tablespoons chopped fresh parsley
2 tablespoons olive oil

RICE STUFFING
1 cup/220 g/7 oz brown rice, cooked
6 spring onions, chopped
1 large avocado, stoned, peeled and mashed
1 tablespoon lemon juice
freshly ground black pepper

1 Loosen skin over breast and tops of legs of poussins, using fingers or the handle of a wooden spoon.

2 Place butter, garlic, chives and parsley in a small bowl and mix well to combine. Spread butter mixture under skin of birds.

3 To make stuffing, place rice, spring onions, avocado and lemon juice in a bowl and mix well to combine. Season to taste with black pepper. Divide stuffing into four equal portions and fill cavities of birds. Tuck wings under body and tie legs firmly together. Place birds in a greased baking dish, brush with oil and bake for 30 minutes or until birds are tender and cooked.

Serves 4

RAINBOW RISOTTO

1 tablespoon vegetable oil
15 g/$^1/_2$ oz butter
1 onion, chopped
$^1/_2$ teaspoon ground turmeric
2 cups/440 g/14 oz rice
4 cups/1 litre/1$^3/_4$ pt vegetable stock
1 small butternut pumpkin or marrow, seeded and chopped
125 g/4 oz fresh or frozen peas
1 small red pepper, chopped
2 zucchini (courgettes), chopped
freshly ground black pepper

1 Heat oil and butter in a large saucepan, add onion and turmeric and cook for 2-3 minutes. Stir in rice and stock, bring to the boil, then reduce heat, cover and simmer for 15 minutes or until rice is tender and most of the liquid is absorbed.

2 Boil, steam or microwave pumpkin and peas, separately, until tender. Drain and add to rice mixture with red pepper and zucchini (courgettes). Cook for 4-5 minutes longer or until heated through. Season to taste with black pepper and serve immediately.

Serves 4

Don't be limited by the vegetables suggested in this recipe. This risotto is just as delicious made with other vegetables, so choose in-season vegetables and those that you and your family enjoy the most. A delicious spring version might include asparagus and snow peas (mangetout).

MAIN MEALS

*Poussin with Rice Stuffing,
Rainbow Risotto*

23

RECIPE COLLECTION

VEGETABLE AND RICE PIE

Oven temperature
220°C, 425°F, Gas 7

250 g/8 oz prepared puff pastry
1 egg, lightly beaten with
1 tablespoon water
1 tablespoon sesame seeds

VEGETABLE AND RICE FILLING
30 g/1 oz butter
1 teaspoon ground turmeric
1 teaspoon ground cumin
1 teaspoon ground coriander
1 onion, chopped
1/2 red pepper, chopped
1 small carrot, chopped
1 stalk celery, chopped
1 zucchini (courgette), chopped
1/2 cup/100 g/3 1/2 oz rice, cooked
2 eggs, lightly beaten
freshly ground black pepper

1 To make filling, melt butter in a large frying pan, add turmeric, cumin, coriander and onion and cook for 5 minutes or until onion is soft. Add red pepper, carrot, celery and zucchini (courgette) and cook for 5 minutes longer. Remove pan from heat, add rice and eggs and mix to combine. Season to taste with black pepper.

2 Divide pastry into two equal portions and roll out each portion to a 25 cm/10 in square. Using a 23 cm/9 in dinner plate or cake tin as a guide cut out two circles. Place one circle on a baking tray lined with nonstick baking paper. Top with filling, spreading out evenly with a fork, leaving a 2.5 cm/1 in border. Moisten border with egg mixture and top with remaining pastry circle.

3 Press edges together firmly to seal. Knock back edges using your finger and a knife to make a decorative scalloped edge.

4 Pierce top of pie several times with a fork, brush with remaining egg mixture, sprinkle with sesame seeds and bake for 15-20 minutes or until pastry is crisp and golden.

Serves 4

Any leftover cooked vegetables can be used in this pie. For a completely different flavour you might like to use fresh or dried mixed herbs in place of the spices.

'This pie is also delicious made with brown rice or a mixture of brown, white and wild rice.'

*Vegetable and Rice Pie,
Vegetable Chilli*

Vegetable Chilli

MAIN MEALS

1 large eggplant (aubergine), cut into 1 cm/½ in cubes
salt
4 tablespoons olive oil
1 large onion, chopped
1 clove garlic, crushed
1 green pepper, sliced
440 g/14 oz canned tomatoes, undrained and mashed
2 zucchini (courgettes), sliced
1 teaspoon hot chilli powder
½ teaspoon ground cumin
2 tablespoons chopped fresh parsley
500 g/1 lb canned three bean mix
freshly ground black pepper

1 Place eggplant (aubergine) in a colander, sprinkle with salt and set aside to stand for 15-20 minutes. Rinse under cold, running water and pat dry with absorbent kitchen paper.

2 Heat oil in a large frying pan, add eggplant (aubergine) and cook, stirring, for 5 minutes or until soft. Transfer eggplant (aubergine) to a large casserole dish.

3 Add onion, garlic and green pepper to frying pan and cook for 5 minutes or until onion is soft. Stir in tomatoes, zucchini (courgettes), chilli powder, cumin, parsley, beans and black pepper to taste and bring to the boil. Transfer bean mixture to casserole dish with eggplant (aubergine) and bake for 1½ hours or until the skin of the eggplant (aubergine) is tender.

Serves 6

Oven temperature
180°C, 350°F, Gas 4

This filling casserole is delicious served with natural yogurt, grated Parmesan cheese and warmed pitta bread rounds.

RECIPE COLLECTION

RICE WITH CHEESE AND HERBS

8 cups/2 litres/3 1/2 pt water
1 1/2 cups/330 g/10 1/2 oz Arborio, risotto or short grain rice
90 g/3 oz butter, cut into small pieces
2 tablespoons chopped mixed fresh herbs
250 g/8 oz grated mozzarella cheese
60 g/2 oz grated Parmesan cheese
freshly ground black pepper

1 Place water in a large saucepan and bring to the boil. Stir in rice and cook, covered, for 15-20 minutes or until rice is tender. Stir occasionally during cooking to prevent sticking.

2 Drain, then return rice to same pan. Stir in butter and chopped herbs. Fold mozzarella and Parmesan cheeses into rice mixture and season to taste with black pepper. Transfer to a warm serving dish and serve immediately.

Serves 4

Much simpler than a risotto, this dish relies on the quality of the fresh herbs and mozzarella used.

POLENTA AND SALAMI BAKE

4 cups/1 litre/1 3/4 pt water
220 g/7 oz polenta
90 g/3 oz butter, cut into pieces
300 g/9 1/2 oz mushrooms, sliced
freshly ground black pepper
2 x 440 g/14 oz canned tomatoes, drained, seeded and mashed
170 g/5 1/2 oz salami, thinly sliced
60 g/2 oz grated Parmesan cheese

WHITE SAUCE
45 g/1 1/2 oz butter
1 small bay leaf
1/4 cup/30 g/1 oz flour
2 cups/500 mL/16 fl oz milk
pinch ground nutmeg

Oven temperature
220°C, 425 F, Gas 7

1 To make sauce, melt butter in a small saucepan, add bay leaf and stir in flour. Cook over a medium heat, stirring constantly, for 1 minute. Remove pan from heat and gradually whisk in milk. Season to taste with black pepper and nutmeg and cook, stirring constantly, for 5-6 minutes or until sauce boils and thickens. Remove pan from heat, cover surface of sauce with plastic food wrap and set aside.

2 Place water in a large saucepan and bring to the boil. Gradually whisk in polenta, then reduce heat and cook, stirring frequently, for 20 minutes.

3 Melt half the butter pieces in a frying pan, add mushrooms and cook over a low heat for 2-3 minutes. Season to taste with black pepper and set aside.

4 Remove polenta from heat and stir in remaining butter pieces. Spread one-third of the polenta over the base of a greased ovenproof dish. Top with one-third of the mushrooms, one-third of the tomatoes, one-third of the salami and one-third of the sauce. Repeat these layers twice, ending with a final layer of sauce. Sprinkle with Parmesan cheese and bake for 30 minutes. Allow to stand for 5-10 minutes before serving.

Serves 4

In Italy, when polenta is presented baked as a pie it is known as Polenta Pasticciata. There are many different versions – probably as many as there are housewives in northern Italy. This one is easy and sure to draw compliments when served.

Rice with Cheese and Herbs, Polenta and Salami Bake

MAIN MEALS

RECIPE COLLECTION

Quick Meals

Some of the following recipes require beans to be presoaked, but once this is done they are quick to prepare. When cooking rice, beans or grains, cook extra so that you have them on hand to make quick meals such as the ones in this chapter. Cooked rice, beans and grains freeze well or will keep in the refrigerator for 3-4 days.

- Bean Cottage Pie
- Wild Rice Salad
- Pumpkins with Bean Filling
- Vegetable and Rice Patties
- Broccoli and Rice Soufflé
- Lentil Burgers
- Rice Fritters
- Mung Bean Frittata
- Bean-filled Tacos
- Lentil Pockets

Bean Cottage Pie

BEAN COTTAGE PIE

QUICK MEALS

1 tablespoon vegetable oil
2 cloves garlic, crushed
2 leeks, white parts only, sliced
2 large carrots, sliced
440 g/14 oz canned tomatoes, undrained and mashed
440 g/14 oz canned lima or butter beans, drained
freshly ground black pepper
750 g/1 1/2 lb potatoes, cooked and mashed
60 g/2 oz grated tasty cheese (mature Cheddar)

1 Heat oil in a large frying pan, add garlic, leeks and carrots and cook, stirring, for 5 minutes or until leeks are tender. Add tomatoes, bring to the boil, then reduce heat and simmer for 10 minutes or until mixture reduces and thickens. Stir in beans and cook for 3-4 minutes longer. Season to taste with black pepper.

2 Transfer bean mixture to a greased ovenproof dish, top with mashed potato and sprinkle with cheese. Bake for 20 minutes or until top is golden.

Serves 4

Oven temperature
180°C, 350°F, Gas 4

Recent studies have shown that the fibre in legumes is soluble and when eaten in conjunction with a low-fat diet can be helpful in lowering blood cholesterol levels as well as controlling the glucose levels of diabetics.

WILD RICE SALAD

100 g/3 1/2 oz wild rice
100 g/3 1/2 oz white rice
100 g/3 1/2 oz quick-cooking brown rice
3 tablespoons chopped fresh mint
1/2 cup/60 g/2 oz toasted sunflower seeds
2 tablespoons chopped glacé ginger or ginger in syrup, drained
2 kiwi fruit, sliced
1/2 cup/90 g/3 oz sultanas

KIWI FRUIT DRESSING
2 kiwi fruit, chopped
1 tablespoon vegetable oil
1 clove garlic, crushed
1 teaspoon grated fresh ginger
2 teaspoons honey
1 teaspoon lemon juice
freshly ground black pepper

1 Cook wild rice in a large pan of boiling water for 15 minutes. Add white and brown rice and cook for 12 minutes longer or until all rices are tender and the grains of the wild rice have burst. Drain and set aside to cool.

2 Place rice mixture, mint, sunflower seeds, chopped ginger, sliced kiwi fruit and sultanas in a salad bowl.

3 To make dressing, place chopped kiwi fruit, oil, garlic, grated ginger, honey, lemon juice and black pepper to taste in a food processor or blender and process until smooth. Spoon dressing over salad, toss to combine and refrigerate for at least 2 hours before serving.

Serves 6

This colourful rice salad is also delicious made with strawberries in place of the kiwi fruit. Simply replace the sliced kiwi fruit in the salad with 125 g/4 oz quartered strawberries and the kiwi fruit in the dressing with 125 g/ 4 oz chopped strawberries.

RECIPE COLLECTION

PUMPKINS WITH BEAN FILLING

Oven temperature
180°C, 350°F, Gas 4

4 golden nugget pumpkins
BEAN FILLING
15 g/^{1}/$_2$ oz burghul (cracked wheat)
1 tablespoon olive oil
2 cloves garlic, crushed
1 small leek, sliced
60 g/2 oz mushrooms, sliced
315 g/10 oz canned red kidney beans, drained and rinsed
1 tablespoon tomato sauce
2 teaspoons Worcestershire sauce
^{1}/$_2$ teaspoon chilli sauce
freshly ground black pepper
90 g/3 oz grated mozzarella cheese

1 Cut tops from pumpkins and scoop out seeds. Bake or microwave pumpkins until just tender. Drain off any liquid that accumulates during cooking and place pumpkins in a lightly greased baking dish.

2 To make filling, soak burghul (cracked wheat) in water for 30 minutes. Drain and set aside. Heat oil in a large frying pan, add garlic, leek and mushrooms and cook, stirring, over a medium heat for 4-5 minutes.

3 Stir in beans, tomato sauce, Worcestershire sauce, chilli sauce and burghul and cook for 3-4 minutes longer or until heated through. Season to taste with black pepper.

4 Divide filling evenly between pumpkins, sprinkle with cheese and bake for 10 minutes or until cheese melts.

Serves 4

Choose the smallest pumpkins you can find for this tasty recipe. If the pumpkins are more than a one-serve size you can use two pumpkins and halve them after cooking or, alternatively, use a larger pumpkin and cut into quarters before serving. This bean filling is also delicious used to stuff a large marrow.

VEGETABLE AND RICE PATTIES

^{3}/$_4$ cup/170 g/5^1/$_2$ oz brown rice, cooked
^{3}/$_4$ cup/30 g/1 oz unprocessed bran
^{3}/$_4$ cup/90 g/3 oz flour
1 onion, grated
1 clove garlic, crushed
1 teaspoon grated fresh ginger
250 g/8 oz canned sweet corn kernels, drained
1 carrot, grated
1 zucchini (courgette), grated
3 tablespoons toasted pine nuts
2 tablespoons peanut butter
2 teaspoons soy sauce
3 tablespoons natural yogurt
2 egg whites
1^1/$_2$ cups/185 g/6 oz dried breadcrumbs
2 tablespoons olive oil

1 Place rice, bran, flour, onion, garlic, ginger, sweet corn, carrot, zucchini (courgette) and pine nuts in a bowl and mix to combine. Place peanut butter, soy sauce, yogurt and egg whites in a food processor or blender and process to combine. Add peanut butter mixture to rice mixture and mix well.

2 Shape rice mixture into sixteen patties and coat with breadcrumbs. Heat oil in a nonstick frying pan and cook patties for 5 minutes each side or until golden and cooked through. Drain on absorbent kitchen paper.

Serves 8

Brown rice has only the inedible outer husk removed. The rice retains its bran layer and so is high in vitamin B. Brown rice has a coarser, nuttier texture and flavour than white rice. It is available in both long and short grain varieties.

*Pumpkins with Bean Filling,
Vegetable and Rice Patties,
Wild Rice Salad*

QUICK MEALS

31

RECIPE COLLECTION

BROCCOLI AND RICE SOUFFLE

Oven temperature
180°C, 350°F, Gas 4

For the best volume have egg whites at room temperature before beating. Egg whites for a soufflé should be beaten until they are stiff but not dry.

125 g/4 oz broccoli, cut into small florets
15 g/½ oz butter
½ onion, chopped
2 tablespoons flour
1 cup/250 mL/8 fl oz hot milk
¼ teaspoon ground nutmeg
freshly ground black pepper
60 g/2 oz grated tasty cheese (mature Cheddar)
⅓ cup/75 g/2½ oz rice, cooked
3 eggs, separated

1 Boil, steam or microwave broccoli until tender. Drain and refresh under cold, running water. Drain again and set aside.

2 Melt butter in a small saucepan, add onion and cook for 2 minutes. Stir in flour and cook, stirring constantly, for 2 minutes longer. Remove pan from heat and gradually whisk in hot milk. Return pan to heat and cook, stirring constantly, for 5 minutes or until sauce boils and thickens. Stir in nutmeg and black pepper to taste.

3 Beat egg yolks into sauce, then add broccoli, cheese and rice and egg yolks to sauce and mix well to combine.

4 Place egg whites in a large bowl and beat until stiff peaks form. Stir one-quarter egg whites into sauce mixture, then carefully fold in remaining egg whites. Spoon soufflé mixture into four lightly greased ¾ cup/185 mL/6 fl oz capacity soufflé dishes and bake for 25 minutes or until soufflés are puffed and golden. Serve immediately.

Serves 4

Left: Broccoli and Rice Soufflé
Right: Lentil Burgers

LENTIL BURGERS

QUICK MEALS

90 g/3 oz red lentils, cooked, drained and mashed
125 g/4 oz instant mashed potato
3/4 cup/185 mL/6 fl oz milk
1 egg, lightly beaten
4 spring onions, chopped
1 clove garlic, crushed
1 teaspoon ground cumin
1 tablespoon chopped fresh coriander
1 teaspoon curry powder
freshly ground black pepper
4 bread rolls, split and toasted

YOGURT MINT SAUCE
1 cup/200 g/6 1/2 oz natural yogurt
1 tablespoon chopped fresh mint

1 To make sauce, place yogurt and mint in a small bowl and mix to combine.

2 Place lentils, mashed potato, milk, egg, spring onions, garlic, cumin, coriander, curry powder and black pepper to taste in a bowl and mix to combine.

3 Shape lentil mixture into eight patties and cook under a preheated grill for 5 minutes each side or until golden and heated through.

4 Place two patties on the bottom half of each bread roll, then top with sauce and top of roll.

Serves 4

For a complete meal, accompany these burgers with carrot ribbons, cucumber slices, onion rings, sliced tomatoes and alfalfa sprouts.
To cook lentils, place them in a saucepan and cover with water or stock. Bring to the boil, then reduce heat and simmer for 30 minutes or until lentils are tender.

RECIPE COLLECTION

RICE FRITTERS

Serve these fritters with hummus or a dipping sauce made of natural yogurt and flavoured with chopped fresh mint and freshly ground black pepper.
Besan flour is made from chickpeas and can be found in Asian specialty food stores and health food shops. Plain flour could be used in place of the besan flour if you wish.

¼ teaspoon chilli powder
1 teaspoon garam masala
½ cup/75 g/2½ oz wholemeal flour
⅔ cup/75 g/2½ oz besan flour
½ cup/100 g/3½ oz brown rice, cooked
2 eggs, lightly beaten
¾ cup/185 mL/6 fl oz milk
4 spring onions, chopped
½ small red pepper, chopped
freshly ground black pepper
vegetable oil for shallow-frying

1 Sift chilli powder, garam masala and wholemeal and besan flours together into a bowl. Mix in rice, then make a well in the centre and gradually stir in eggs and milk. Mix to make a smooth batter, then stir in spring onions, red pepper and black pepper to taste.

2 Heat oil in a large frying pan and cook spoonfuls of batter for 3-4 minutes each side or until golden. Drain on absorbent kitchen paper and serve immediately.

Makes 20

MUNG BEAN FRITTATA

100 g/3½ oz dried mung beans
2 eggs
2 tablespoons vegetable oil
1 onion, sliced
2 potatoes, grated
2 carrots, grated
2 zucchini (courgettes), grated
125 g/4 oz canned sweet corn kernels, drained
3 tablespoons chopped fresh basil
freshly ground black pepper
125 g/4 oz grated tasty cheese (mature Cheddar)

COCONUT CREAM
½ cup/125 mL/4 fl oz coconut milk
1 tablespoon lemon juice
2 tablespoons chopped fresh mint

If commercially made coconut milk is unavailable, you can make it using desiccated coconut and water. To make coconut milk, place 500 g/1 lb desiccated coconut in a bowl and pour over 3 cups/750 mL/1¼ pt boiling water. Leave to stand for 30 minutes, then strain, squeezing the coconut to extract as much liquid as possible. This will make a thick coconut milk. The coconut can be used again to make a weaker coconut milk.

1 Place mung beans in a bowl, pour over boiling water to cover and set aside to soak for 30 minutes. Drain beans and place in a food processor or blender with eggs and process until smooth. Transfer to a large bowl.

2 Heat 1 tablespoon oil in a frying pan, add onion and cook over a low heat for 3-4 minutes. Add potatoes, carrots and zucchini (courgettes) and cook, stirring, for 5 minutes or until vegetables are tender. Remove vegetables from pan and drain on absorbent kitchen paper.

3 Add cooked vegetables, sweet corn, basil and black pepper to taste to bean mixture and mix well to combine.

4 Heat remaining oil in a large nonstick frying pan, add vegetable mixture, sprinkle with cheese and cook over a low heat for 5-8 minutes or until just firm. Place pan under a preheated grill and cook for 3 minutes or until top of frittata is browned.

5 To make Coconut Cream, place coconut milk, lemon juice and mint in a screwtop jar and shake well to combine. Invert frittata onto a serving plate, cut into wedges and serve with Coconut Cream.

Serves 6

*Rice Fritters,
Mung Bean Frittata*

QUICK MEALS

RECIPE COLLECTION

BEAN-FILLED TACOS

Oven temperature
180°C, 350°F, Gas 4

Beans belong to the *Leguminosae* family and are often referred to as legumes or pulses. Beans are the edible seeds of various shrubs and vines. They are left behind after the plant reaches maturity and dries up and withers. These dried seeds or beans are highly nutritious, being rich in both carbohydrate and vegetable protein.

12 taco shells
1 avocado, sliced and brushed with
2 tablespoons lemon juice
125 g/4 oz cottage cheese
¼ lettuce, shredded
1 tomato, chopped
1 tablespoon chilli sauce (optional)

SPICY BEAN FILLING
1 tablespoon vegetable oil
1 onion, chopped
45 g/1½ oz packet taco seasoning
¼ teaspoon chilli powder
1 red pepper, chopped
1 zucchini (courgette), chopped
315 g/10 oz canned red kidney beans, drained
440 g/14 oz canned tomatoes, undrained and mashed
3 tablespoons tomato paste (purée)

1 To make filling, heat oil in a large frying pan, add onion and cook for 5 minutes. Stir in taco seasoning and chilli powder and cook for 1 minute longer.

2 Add red pepper and zucchini (courgette) and cook, stirring, for 3-4 minutes. Stir in beans, mashed tomatoes and tomato paste (purée), bring to simmering and simmer for 10 minutes or until mixture reduces and thickens.

3 Place taco shells on a baking tray and heat in the oven for 5 minutes. Half fill each taco shell with filling, then top with avocado slices and serve immediately with cottage cheese, lettuce, chopped tomato and chilli sauce, if desired.

Serves 4

36

LENTIL POCKETS

200 g/6¹/₂ oz red lentils
15 g/¹/₂ oz butter
1 onion, chopped
2 cloves garlic, crushed
3 carrots, chopped
1 tomato, chopped
1 tablespoon chopped fresh oregano or
1 teaspoon dried oregano
¹/₂ cup/125 mL/4 fl oz water
1 bunch/500 g/1 lb spinach, stalks removed and leaves chopped
1 tablespoon lemon juice
6 large pitta bread rounds, warmed and cut in half

1 Place lentils in a large saucepan, cover with water and bring to the boil. Reduce heat and simmer for 30 minutes or until lentils are tender. Drain and set aside.

2 Melt butter in a large saucepan, add onion and garlic and cook over a medium heat, stirring, for 5 minutes or until onion is soft. Add carrots, tomato, oregano and water and bring to the boil. Reduce heat and simmer for 10 minutes or until carrots are tender.

3 Add spinach, lemon juice and lentils to pan, bring to simmering and simmer for 15 minutes or until mixture reduces and thickens.

4 Spoon lentil mixture into pitta bread pockets and serve immediately.

Serves 6

Above: Lentil Pockets
Left: Bean-filled Tacos

Lentils are used extensively in the cuisines of Europe and India. High in fibre, low in fat and a good source of plant protein, iron, potassium pyridoxine, thiamin and riboflavin, they are an important food for vegetarians.

RECIPE COLLECTION

RISOTTOS

The best rice to use for making a traditional risotto is Arborio or risotto rice. Arborio rice absorbs liquid without becoming soft and it is this special quality that makes it so suitable for risottos. A risotto made in the traditional way, where liquid is added a little at a time as the rice cooks, will take 20-30 minutes to cook.

Creamy Mushroom Risotto

Artichoke Risotto

Prawn Risotto

Moulded Tomato Risotto

Risotto with Cheese with Two Variations

Vegetable and Bean Risotto

Creamy Mushroom Risotto

Creamy Mushroom Risotto

RISOTTOS

30 g/1 oz dried mushrooms
boiling water
60 g/2 oz butter
1 onion, chopped
2 cloves garlic, crushed
1 cup/220 g/7 oz Arborio or risotto rice
250 g/8 oz button mushrooms, sliced
2 cups/500 mL/16 fl oz hot chicken or vegetable stock
3 tablespoons chopped fresh parsley
3 tablespoons grated Parmesan cheese
freshly ground black pepper

1 Place mushrooms in a bowl and cover with boiling water. Set aside to soak for 20 minutes or until mushrooms are tender. Drain, remove stalks if necessary and chop mushrooms.

2 Melt butter in a large saucepan, add onion and garlic and cook for 5 minutes or until onion is soft. Add rice, prepared dried mushrooms and button mushrooms and cook, stirring, for 1 minute.

3 Stir in ¹/₂ cup/125 mL/4 fl oz hot stock and cook, stirring constantly, until liquid is absorbed. Continue adding stock, a ¹/₂ cup/125 mL/4 fl oz at a time, stirring constantly and allowing stock to be absorbed before adding any more. Stir in parsley, Parmesan cheese and black pepper to taste and serve immediately.

Serves 4

Arborio rice is an Italian short grain rice from the Po Valley. It is recognisable by the distinctive white spot on each kernel. If Arborio rice is unavailable, short grain rice can be used instead.

Artichoke Risotto

60 g/2 oz butter
1 onion, chopped
1¹/₂ cups/330 g/10¹/₂ oz Arborio or risotto rice
2 cups/500 mL/16 fl oz chicken stock
¹/₂ cup/125 mL/4 fl oz dry white wine
440 g/14 oz canned artichoke hearts, drained and liquid reserved
2 tablespoons chopped fresh parsley
4 thick slices ham, cut into strips
60 g/2 oz grated Parmesan cheese
4 cherry tomatoes, quartered
freshly ground black pepper

1 Melt butter in a large frying pan, add onion and cook for 5 minutes or until soft.

2 Add rice to pan and cook, stirring frequently, for 5 minutes. Combine stock, wine and reserved artichoke liquid. The total amount of liquid should equal 3¹/₂ cups/875 mL/1¹/₂ pt. Top up with additional stock, if necessary. Pour one-third of the liquid over the rice and cook over a low heat, stirring, until liquid is absorbed. Continue adding liquid a little at a time and cook, stirring frequently, until all liquid is absorbed.

3 Cut artichokes into quarters. Fold artichokes, parsley, ham, Parmesan cheese and tomatoes into rice. Season to taste with black pepper and serve immediately.

Serves 4

Try using asparagus as a substitute for the artichokes in this aromatic risotto.

RECIPE COLLECTION

Prawn Risotto

125 g/4 oz butter
2 leeks, white part only, sliced
2 cloves garlic, crushed
500 g/1 lb uncooked large prawns, shelled and deveined, tails left intact
1½ cups/330 g/10½ oz basmati rice
½ cup/125 mL/4 fl oz dry white wine
3½ cups/875 mL/1½ pt boiling fish or chicken stock
3 tablespoons chopped fresh basil
freshly ground black pepper

This recipe uses the cooking method for risotto but uses the fragrant Oriental rice basmati. Traditionally grown in the Himalayan foothills, basmati rice is used extensively in Indian cooking. Its name means 'fragrance' and as the rice cooks, you will notice a distinctive aroma.

1 Melt 60 g/2 oz butter in a large frying pan, add leeks and garlic and cook, stirring, for 5 minutes or until leeks are tender. Add prawns and cook for 3-4 minutes or until prawns just change colour. Remove pan from heat and set aside.

2 Melt remaining butter in a large saucepan, add rice and cook, stirring constantly, for 2 minutes. Stir in wine and cook until liquid is absorbed. Stir in ½ cup/125 mL/4 fl oz boiling stock and cook, stirring constantly, until liquid is absorbed. Continue adding stock a ½ cup/125 mL/4 fl oz at a time, stirring constantly and allowing stock to be absorbed before adding any more. Stir in prawn mixture, basil and black pepper to taste and cook for 3-4 minutes longer or until heated through. Serve immediately.

Serves 4

Left: Prawn Risotto
Below: Moulded Tomato Risotto

RISOTTOS

MOULDED TOMATO RISOTTO

3 tablespoons olive oil
2 onions, chopped
2 cups/440 g/14 oz quick-cooking brown rice
440 g/14 oz canned tomatoes, undrained and mashed
3 tablespoons tomato paste (purée)
4 cups/1 litre/1³/₄ pt boiling chicken stock
90 g/3 oz butter
125 g/4 oz grated Parmesan cheese
2 tablespoons chopped fresh basil
freshly ground black pepper

1 Heat oil in a large frying pan, add onions and cook over a medium heat for 10 minutes or until golden. Stir in rice and cook for 2 minutes longer.

2 Add tomatoes, tomato paste (purée) and stock and cook, stirring frequently, until liquid is absorbed and rice is cooked.

3 Stir in butter, Parmesan cheese, basil and black pepper to taste. Spoon rice mixture into a well-greased ovenproof bowl, cover and bake for 10-15 minutes. Allow to stand 5-10 minutes before turning out and serving.

Serves 6

Oven temperature
200°C, 400°F, Gas 6

This moulded risotto looks attractive when served garnished with zucchini (courgette) ribbons. To make, cut long thin slices from top to base of zucchini (courgette), using a vegetable peeler.

RECIPE COLLECTION

RISOTTO WITH CHEESE

5 cups/1.25 litres/2 pt chicken or beef stock
2 tablespoons vegetable oil
45 g/1 1/2 oz butter
1 small onion, chopped
1 1/2 cups/330 g/10 1/2 oz Arborio or risotto rice
60 g/2 oz grated Parmesan cheese
freshly ground black pepper

1 Place stock in a large saucepan and bring to the boil. Reduce heat and simmer.

2 Heat oil and 30 g/1 oz butter in a separate saucepan, add onion and cook over a low heat for 5-6 minutes or until lightly browned. Add rice and cook, stirring, for 1-2 minutes. This will coat the grains well with the butter mixture. Pour in 3/4 cup/185 mL/6 fl oz boiling stock and stir over medium heat until liquid is absorbed.

3 Continue cooking in this way until all the stock is used and rice is just tender; this will take 18-20 minutes. Stir frequently during cooking to prevent sticking.

4 Stir in Parmesan cheese, remaining butter and black pepper to taste. Serve immediately.

Serves 4

This traditional Italian risotto is sure to be popular. Use the variations as a guide to creating your own favourite flavour combinations – almost anything you like can be used to make delicious risottos. The secret to a good risotto is to keep the flavours simple and not to use too many different ingredients.

VARIATIONS

Risotto with Asparagus and Bacon: For this variation you will require the ingredients for Risotto with Cheese, plus 2 rashers bacon, chopped and 500 g/1 lb fresh asparagus. Make up Risotto with Cheese, cooking the bacon with the onion. Cook the asparagus in the boiling stock. When tender, remove and set aside to cool, then cut into 5 cm/2 in pieces. Fold into risotto just prior to serving.

Risotto with Spinach and Herbs: For this variation you will require the ingredients for Risotto with Cheese, plus 2 cloves garlic, crushed, 1 bunch/500 g/ 1 lb spinach, 1 tablespoon finely chopped fresh basil, and 1 tablespoon finely chopped fresh oregano or 1 teaspoon dried oregano. Make up Risotto with Cheese, cooking the garlic with the onion. Boil, steam or microwave spinach until tender and chop finely. Fold cooked spinach, basil and oregano into cooked risotto.

Vegetable and Bean Risotto

RISOTTOS

1 tablespoon olive oil
1 teaspoon poppy seeds
1 teaspoon mustard seeds
1 cup/220 g/7 oz long grain rice
¼ teaspoon chilli powder
1 teaspoon ground turmeric
1 teaspoon ground cumin
1 teaspoon ground coriander
1 cup/250 mL/8 fl oz water
1 eggplant (aubergine), cut into 5 mm/¼ in cubes
½ red pepper, chopped
315 g/10 oz canned lima or butter beans, drained and rinsed
1½ cups/375 mL/12 fl oz tomato purée
1½ cups/375 mL/12 fl oz chicken stock
½ cup/125 mL/4 fl oz coconut milk
1 tablespoon chopped fresh coriander
freshly ground black pepper

1 Heat oil in a large frying pan, add poppy and mustard seeds and cook until they begin to pop. Add rice and cook, stirring, for 5 minutes.

2 Place chilli powder, turmeric, cumin, ground coriander and a little water in a small bowl and mix to form a paste. Stir spice mixture, eggplant (aubergine), red pepper and beans into rice mixture and cook, stirring, for 5 minutes.

3 Place remaining water, tomato purée, stock and coconut milk in a bowl and whisk to combine. Add to rice mixture, bring to simmering and simmer for 30-40 minutes or until most of the liquid is absorbed and rice is cooked. Stir in fresh coriander and black pepper to taste. Serve immediately.

Serves 6

The combination of rice and beans in this Oriental-flavoured risotto makes a perfectly balanced vegetarian meal.

RECIPE COLLECTION

VEGETARIAN

Rice, beans and grains should form the basis of a balanced vegetarian diet. These foods supply much of the protein, vitamins and minerals that non-vegetarians obtain from meat. While there are many meatless dishes in this book, the recipes in this chapter have been especially chosen for those following a vegetarian diet.

Lentil Salad

Red Hot Beans

Cheesy Brown Rice Pie

Bean Patties with Avocado Sauce

Spicy Vegetable Loaf

Vegetable and Lentil Curry

*Lentil Salad,
Red Hot Beans*

LENTIL SALAD

VEGETARIAN

200 g/6 1/2 oz red lentils
200 g/6 1/2 oz yellow lentils
6 cups/1.5 litres/2 1/2 pt vegetable stock
1 teaspoon cumin seeds
2 tomatoes, diced
2 stalks celery, sliced
1/2 green pepper, diced
1/2 red pepper, diced
1 small onion, chopped
1 small avocado, stoned, peeled and chopped
2 tablespoons snipped fresh chives
SPICY DRESSING
1/4 teaspoon ground coriander
1/4 teaspoon ground turmeric
pinch chilli powder
1 clove garlic, crushed
4 tablespoons cider vinegar
1 tablespoon olive oil
freshly ground black pepper

1   Place red and yellow lentils, stock and cumin seeds in a saucepan and bring to the boil. Reduce heat and simmer for 20 minutes or until lentils are tender. Drain and set aside to cool.

2   Place cold lentils, tomatoes, celery, green and red pepper, onion and avocado in a large salad bowl.

3   To make dressing, place coriander, turmeric, chilli powder, garlic, vinegar, oil and black pepper to taste in a screwtop jar and shake well to combine. Spoon dressing over salad and toss to combine. Sprinkle with chives and serve immediately.

Serves 6

Dried peas, beans and lentils are often avoided because they cause embarrassing flatulence (wind). This can be considerably reduced by discarding soaking water, rinsing beans, and adding fresh water for cooking. The flatulence is caused by certain food components in legumes, which are not fully digested, and end up being broken down into gases in the bowel.

RED HOT BEANS

250 g/8 oz dried red kidney beans
1 eggplant (aubergine), diced
1 red pepper, cut into strips
1 onion, sliced
1 clove garlic, crushed
4 large tomatoes, skinned and chopped
2 tablespoons tomato purée
2 teaspoons chilli sauce
1 cup/250 mL/8 fl oz water
freshly ground pepper
2 tablespoons chopped fresh coriander

1   Place beans in a large bowl, cover with water and set aside to soak overnight, then drain.

2   Place beans, eggplant (aubergine), red pepper, onion, garlic, tomatoes, tomato purée, chilli sauce and water in a large saucepan and bring to the boil. Boil for 15 minutes then reduce heat and simmer, stirring occasionally, for 1 hour or until beans are tender. Season to taste with black pepper and sprinkle with coriander.

Serves 4

The hotness of Red Hot Beans can be altered according to taste. If you are unsure, carefully add chilli sauce a little at a time, tasting until it is right. Serve with bowls of natural yogurt.

RECIPE COLLECTION

Cheesy Brown Rice Pie

Oven temperature
190°C, 375°F, Gas 5

To cook brown rice in the microwave, place 1 cup/ 220 g/7 oz rice and 3 cups/ 750 mL/1¼ pt water or stock in a large microwave-safe dish. Cook, uncovered, on HIGH (100%) for 30 minutes or until all the liquid is absorbed and the rice is tender.

¾ cup/170 g/5½ oz brown rice, cooked
250 g/8 oz grated tasty cheese (mature Cheddar)
4 tablespoons grated Parmesan cheese
2 spring onions, chopped
2 zucchini (courgettes), grated
1 red pepper, diced
315 g/10 oz canned asparagus cuts, drained
3 tablespoons pine nuts, toasted
3 eggs, lightly beaten
1 cup/200 g/6½ oz natural yogurt
freshly ground black pepper

1 Place rice, tasty cheese (mature Cheddar), Parmesan cheese, spring onions, zucchini (courgettes), red pepper, asparagus, pine nuts, eggs, yogurt and black pepper to taste in a bowl and mix to combine.

2 Spoon rice mixture into a greased, deep-sided 23 cm/9 in springform tin and bake for 40 minutes or until firm. Allow to stand for 5 minutes in tin before turning out and serving. Serve cut into wedges.

Serves 6

Left: Cheesy Brown Rice Pie
Below: Bean Patties with Avocado Sauce

VEGETARIAN

BEAN PATTIES WITH AVOCADO SAUCE

2 x 315 g/10 oz canned lima or butter beans, drained and rinsed
1 large carrot, grated
3 cups/185 g/6 oz breadcrumbs, made from stale bread
2 eggs, lightly beaten
4 tablespoons tomato sauce
2 tablespoons snipped fresh chives
freshly ground black pepper
1 cup/125 g/4 oz dried breadcrumbs
2 tablespoons vegetable oil

AVOCADO SAUCE
1/2 cup/125 g/4 oz sour cream
1/2 avocado, mashed
2 teaspoons lemon juice
pinch chilli powder

1 To make patties, place half the beans in a bowl and mash. Add carrot, breadcrumbs made from stale bread, eggs, tomato sauce, chives, black pepper to taste and remaining beans and mix well to combine. Shape bean mixture into twelve patties, using wet hands. Roll patties in dried breadcrumbs to coat, place on a tray or plate lined with plastic food wrap, cover and refrigerate for 30 minutes.

2 Heat oil in a nonstick frying pan and cook patties for 4-5 minutes each side or until golden and heated through.

3 To make sauce, place sour cream, avocado, lemon juice and chilli powder in a small saucepan and heat until just warm. Serve sauce with patties.

Makes 12 patties

Leftover patties can be frozen between sheets of plastic food wrap in an airtight freezerproof container or sealed freezer bag. Defrost patties at room temperature for 1 1/2-2 hours and serve cold. Or reheat in a nonstick frying pan over a medium heat for 3-4 minutes, or in the oven at 180°C/350°F/Gas 4 for 4-5 minutes or until heated. To defrost and reheat in the microwave, defrost 1 pattie on DEFROST (30%) for 3-4 minutes, then heat on HIGH (100%) for 1-2 minutes.

RECIPE COLLECTION

Oven temperature
180 C, 350 F, Gas 4

Legumes supply valuable amounts of B group vitamins, especially vitamin B, B6, niacin and folic acid. Their iron content is fairly high, but occurs in an inorganic form, not well absorbed by the human body. Eating a food high in vitamin C (such as orange juice or a salad) at the same meal as legumes increases the absorption of iron.

When cooking beans and rice, cook extra as these can be frozen and added to dishes as required.

SPICY VEGETABLE LOAF

1 tablespoon olive oil
1 clove garlic, crushed
1 onion, chopped
$1/2$ teaspoon chilli powder
$1/2$ teaspoon ground cumin
$1/2$ teaspoon ground coriander
$1/2$ teaspoon ground turmeric
500 g/1 lb red lentils
1 carrot, grated
1 large potato, grated
440 g/14 oz canned tomatoes, undrained and mashed
2 cups/500 mL/16 fl oz vegetable stock
3 egg whites
$1^1/2$ cups/140 g/$4^1/2$ oz rolled oats
freshly ground black pepper

1 Heat oil in a large frying pan, add garlic, onion, chilli powder, cumin, coriander and turmeric and cook for 4-5 minutes or until onion is soft.

2 Add lentils, carrot, potato, tomatoes and stock and bring to the boil. Reduce heat, cover and simmer for 30 minutes or until lentils are tender. Remove pan from heat and set aside to cool slightly.

3 Place egg whites in a bowl and beat until stiff peaks form. Fold egg whites into lentil mixture.

4 Stir rolled oats into lentil mixture and season to taste with black pepper. Spoon into a lightly greased 11 x 21 cm/$4^1/2$ x $8^1/2$ in loaf tin and bake for 1 hour.

Serves 6

VEGETABLE AND LENTIL CURRY

1 tablespoon olive oil
1 onion, sliced
1 clove garlic, crushed
1 teaspoon ground cumin
1 teaspoon ground coriander
1 teaspoon ground turmeric
2 carrots, sliced
100 g/$3^1/2$ oz red lentils
440 g/14 oz canned tomatoes, undrained and mashed
$1^1/2$ cups/375 mL/12 fl oz vegetable stock or water
1 teaspoon chilli sauce, or according to taste
500 g/1 lb pumpkin or potatoes, cut into 2 cm/$3/4$ in cubes
$1/2$ cauliflower, cut into florets
2 tablespoons blanched almonds
freshly ground black pepper
4 tablespoons natural yogurt

1 Heat oil in a large saucepan, add onion, garlic, cumin, coriander, turmeric and carrots and cook for 5 minutes or until onion is soft.

2 Stir in lentils, tomatoes and stock or water and bring to the boil. Reduce heat, cover and simmer for 15 minutes.

3 Add chilli sauce, pumpkin and cauliflower and cook for 15-20 minutes longer or until pumpkin is tender. Stir in almonds and black pepper to taste. To serve, ladle curry into bowls and top with a spoonful of yogurt.

Serves 4

*Spicy Vegetable Loaf,
Vegetable and Lentil Curry*

VEGETARIAN

RECIPE COLLECTION

SALADS

Salads made with rice, beans and grains make satisfying and substantial side dishes. When these ingredients are teamed with fish or meat you have a wonderful main course. So next time you are looking for a warm weather main dish why not try Seafood Paella Salad or Tuna Bean Salad?

Seafood Paella Salad

Warm Rice Salad

Marinated Bean Salad

Tuna Bean Salad

Bean and Bacon Salad

Golden Grain Salad

Bean and Artichoke Salad

Seafood Paella Salad

Seafood Paella Salad

SALADS

4 cups/1 litre/1 3/4 pt chicken stock
500 g/1 lb uncooked large prawns
1 uncooked lobster tail (optional)
500 g/1 lb mussels in shells, cleaned
2 tablespoons olive oil
1 onion, chopped
2 ham steaks, cut into 1 cm/1/2 in cubes
2 cups/440 g/14 oz rice
1/2 teaspoon ground turmeric
125 g/4 oz fresh or frozen peas
1 red pepper, diced

GARLIC DRESSING
1/2 cup/125 mL/4 fl oz olive oil
1/4 cup/60 mL/2 fl oz white wine vinegar
3 tablespoons mayonnaise
2 cloves garlic, crushed
2 tablespoons chopped fresh parsley
freshly ground black pepper

1 Place stock in a large saucepan and bring to the boil. Add prawns and cook for 1-2 minutes or until prawns change colour. Remove and set aside. Add lobster tail and cook for 5 minutes or until lobster changes colour and is cooked. Remove and set aside. Add mussels and cook until shells open – discard any mussels that do not open after 5 minutes. Remove and set aside. Strain stock and reserve. Peel and devein prawns, leaving tails intact. Refrigerate seafood until just prior to serving.

2 Heat oil in a large saucepan, add onion and cook for 4-5 minutes or until soft. Add ham, rice and turmeric and cook, stirring, for 2 minutes. Add reserved stock and bring to the boil. Reduce heat, cover and simmer for 15 minutes or until liquid is absorbed and rice is cooked and dry. Stir in peas and red pepper and set aside to cool. Cover and refrigerate for at least 2 hours.

3 To make dressing, place oil, vinegar, mayonnaise, garlic, parsley and black pepper to taste in a food processor or blender and process to combine.

4 To serve, place seafood and rice in a large salad bowl, spoon over dressing and toss to combine.

Serves 8

This attractive, special occasion salad is just right for an 'al fresco' luncheon. Serve with a tossed green salad, crusty bread and a dry white wine then follow with a platter of summer fruit for a meal to remember.

'Rice is a great carbohydrate food for weight-watchers; 155 g/5 oz cooked white rice provides only 670 kJ/160 Calories.'

RECIPE COLLECTION

Warm Rice Salad

1 tablespoon olive oil
3 tablespoons white wine vinegar
2 tablespoons orange juice
2 cloves garlic, crushed
2 stalks celery, chopped
3 tablespoons chopped sun-dried tomatoes
60 g/2 oz button mushrooms, sliced
2 baby squash, quartered, or 2 zucchini (courgettes), sliced
60 g/2 oz fresh or frozen peas
440 g/14 oz canned artichokes, drained and halved
3/4 cup/170 g/5 1/2 oz rice, cooked
2 carrots, grated
8 black olives, pitted and sliced
freshly ground black pepper

1 Heat oil in a large frying pan, add vinegar, orange juice and garlic and cook for 1 minute.

2 Add celery, sun-dried tomatoes, mushrooms, squash or zucchini (courgettes) and peas and cook for 3 minutes. Stir in artichokes, rice, carrots and olives and cook, stirring, for 4-5 minutes or until heated through. Season to taste with black pepper. Serve warm.

Serves 4

This warm salad will add a Mediterranean feel to any meal. It is delicious served with grilled meat or poultry.

Left: Warm Rice Salad
Below: Marinated Bean Salad

SALADS

MARINATED BEAN SALAD

125 g/4 oz green beans, cut in half
2 zucchini (courgettes), cut into matchsticks
1 carrot, cut into matchsticks
250 g/8 oz canned red kidney beans, drained and rinsed
250 g/8 oz canned chickpeas, drained and rinsed
250 g/8 oz canned pinto beans, drained and rinsed
125 g/4 oz water chestnuts, drained
1 red pepper, cut into strips
2 tablespoons chopped fresh parsley
1 tablespoon chopped fresh basil

ITALIAN DRESSING
1/4 cup/60 mL/2 fl oz olive oil
2 tablespoons red wine vinegar
1 clove garlic, crushed
freshly ground black pepper

1 Boil, steam or microwave green beans, zucchini (courgettes) and carrot, separately, until just tender. Drain and refresh under cold running water.

2 To make dressing, place oil, vinegar, garlic and black pepper to taste in a screwtop jar and shake well to combine.

3 Place cooked vegetables, red kidney beans, chickpeas, pinto beans, water chestnuts, pepper, parsley and basil in a large salad bowl. Spoon over dressing and toss to combine. Cover and refrigerate for 4-6 hours or overnight. Just prior to serving, toss again.

Serves 6

Canned beans are a quick and nutritious alternative to dried beans. There is some loss of B vitamins during canning, but this is not significant. A couple of cans of beans in your cupboard are always a handy standby for an easy, no-fuss, high-fibre meal.

RECIPE COLLECTION

Right: Tuna Bean Salad
Far right: Bean and Bacon Salad

Tuna Bean Salad

375 g/12 oz dried haricot beans
1 onion, halved
440 g/14 oz canned tuna, drained and flaked
4 spring onions, chopped
1 red pepper, diced
4 tablespoons chopped fresh parsley
4 tablespoons olive oil
2 tablespoons cider vinegar
freshly ground black pepper

1 Place beans in a large bowl, cover with water and set aside to soak overnight, then drain. Place beans and onion in a saucepan with enough water to cover and bring to the boil. Boil for 10 minutes, then reduce heat and simmer for 1 hour or until beans are tender. Remove onion and discard, drain beans and set aside to cool.

2 Place beans, tuna, spring onions, red pepper and parsley in a salad bowl.

3 Place oil, vinegar and black pepper to taste in a screwtop jar and shake well to combine. Pour dressing over bean mixture and toss to combine. Serve immediately.

Serves 6

You might like to make this salad using chicken in place of the tuna. For a quick version use a can of haricot beans instead of the dried ones. Simply drain and rinse the beans, then assemble the salad as described in the recipe.

Bean and Bacon Salad

1 small head broccoli, broken into small florets
185 g/6 oz snow peas (mangetout)
6 rashers bacon, cut into strips
440 g/14 oz canned lima or butter beans, drained and rinsed
1 tablespoon chopped fresh parsley

FRENCH DRESSING
1/4 cup/60 mL/2 fl oz olive oil
1 tablespoon cider vinegar
1 teaspoon Dijon mustard
freshly ground black pepper

1 Boil, steam or microwave broccoli and snow peas (mangetout), separately, until just tender. Drain and place in a large salad bowl.

2 Cook bacon in a frying pan, stirring constantly, for 4-5 minutes or until lightly browned. Remove and drain on absorbent kitchen paper.

3 To make dressing, place oil, vinegar, mustard and black pepper to taste in a screwtop jar and shake well to combine.

4 Add bacon, beans and parsley to salad bowl. Pour over dressing and toss to combine. Serve immediately.

Serves 4

This warm salad makes an interesting starter to a winter meal.

RECIPE COLLECTION

GOLDEN GRAIN SALAD

1 cup/220 g/7 oz brown rice, cooked
1 cup/200 g/6^1/$_2$ oz barley, cooked
^{1}/$_2$ cup/60 g/2 oz couscous, cooked
440 g/14 oz canned sweet corn kernels, drained
1 green pepper, cut into strips
1 carrot, cut into matchsticks
2 stalks celery, cut into matchsticks
1 zucchini (courgette), cut into matchsticks

ORANGE DRESSING
^{1}/$_2$ cup/125 mL/4 fl oz orange juice
2 teaspoons wholegrain mustard
1 teaspoon finely grated fresh ginger
freshly ground black pepper

1 Place rice, barley, couscous, sweet corn, green pepper, carrot, celery and zucchini (courgette) in a large salad bowl.

2 To make dressing, place orange juice, mustard, ginger and black pepper to taste in a screwtop jar and shake well to combine. Pour dressing over salad and toss to combine.

Serves 4

Keep a selection of cooked rice, beans and grains in the refrigerator then you will always have carbohydrate-rich food that can be made into a salad in minutes.

BEAN AND ARTICHOKE SALAD

250 g/8 oz green beans, cut into 2 cm/^{3}/$_4$ in pieces
1 red pepper, cut into thin strips
250 g/8 oz canned lima or butter beans, drained and rinsed
440 g/14 oz canned artichoke hearts, drained and halved
2 tablespoons olive oil
4 tablespoons vinegar
freshly ground black pepper

1 Boil, steam or microwave green beans until just tender. Drain and refresh under cold running water. Set aside.

2 Place red pepper strips in a bowl of iced water for 20 minutes or until curled.

3 Place green beans, red pepper, lima or butter beans, artichoke hearts, oil, vinegar and black pepper to taste in a bowl and toss to combine.

Serves 4

Did you know that in Japan roasted soya beans are used as 'beans of good fortune'? The beans are scattered throughout the house and tossed through open windows to reject bad luck and to welcome good fortune.

Bean and Artichoke Salad

SALADS

RECIPE COLLECTION

SIDE DISHES

The recipes in this chapter show you inspiring ways to serve rice and beans as side dishes. So the next time you are looking for an alternative to plain potatoes or rice, why not try Pickled Tomatoes and Beans or Rose-scented Saffron Rice?

Spiced Broccoli Pilau

Rose-scented Saffron Rice

Pilau with Vegetables

Lontong

Pickled Tomatoes and Beans

Chilli Bean Potatoes

Spiced Broccoli Pilau

SPICED BROCCOLI PILAU

SIDE DISHES

60 g/2 oz butter
1 onion, chopped
1 clove garlic, crushed
1 tablespoon cumin seeds
2 cinnamon sticks
2 bay leaves
1 teaspoon ground cardamom
1 head broccoli, broken into small florets
1/3 cup/90 mL/3 fl oz water
1 1/2 cups/330 g/10 1/2 oz basmati rice, cooked
125 g/4 oz roasted cashew nuts
2 oranges, segmented

1 Melt butter in a large frying pan, add onion and cook for 4-5 minutes or until onion is soft. Stir in garlic, cumin seeds, cinnamon, bay leaves and cardamom and cook for 1 minute.

2 Add broccoli and water, cover and cook for 5 minutes or until broccoli is tender.

3 Stir in rice, cashew nuts and oranges and cook for 5 minutes longer or until heated through.

Serves 6

A pilau, pilaff, pilaf, pilao or pilaw are all the same sort of rice dish – it just depends what country you are in. A pilau consists of rice and spices cooked in stock and may or may not include meat, fish or poultry. This type of dish is common throughout India and the Middle East. It makes a delicious light meal or accompaniment.

ROSE-SCENTED SAFFRON RICE

500 g/1 lb basmati rice, washed
60 g/2 oz ghee or clarified butter
1 onion, chopped
250 g/8 oz minced lean lamb
1/2 teaspoon mixed spice
60 g/2 oz currants
1/2 teaspoon powdered saffron
2 tablespoons rosewater
4 cups/1 litre/1 3/4 pt chicken stock
60 g/2 oz blanched almonds, toasted

1 Place rice in a large bowl, cover with cold water and set aside to stand for 30 minutes.

2 Heat ghee or butter in a large heavy-based frying pan over a medium heat, add onion and cook for 5 minutes or until soft. Increase heat, add lamb and cook until browned. Stir in mixed spice and currants and cook for 1 minute longer. Remove pan from heat, set aside and keep warm.

3 Place saffron and rosewater in a cup and mix to combine. Place chicken stock and 2 teaspoons rosewater mixture in a large saucepan and bring to the boil. Drain rice, add to stock mixture and bring back to the boil, stirring occasionally. Reduce heat, cover and simmer for 30 minutes.

4 Mix meat mixture into rice, remove pan from heat, cover and set aside to stand for 5 minutes before serving. To serve, sprinkle with remaining rosewater mixture and top with almonds.

Serves 6

To clarify butter, place it in a small saucepan and melt it over a low heat. Skim the foam from the surface of the butter, then slowly pour the butter into a bowl, leaving behind the milky-white solids. Ghee is a type of clarified butter.

RECIPE COLLECTION

PILAU WITH VEGETABLES

2 eggplant (aubergines), cut into
2.5 cm/1 in cubes
salt
¼ cup/60 mL/2 fl oz olive oil
1 onion, sliced
440 g/14 oz canned tomatoes, drained
and mashed
2 tablespoons chopped fresh parsley
1 tablespoon chopped fresh mint
500 g/1 lb long grain rice
3 cups/750 mL/1¼ pt chicken stock

1 Sprinkle eggplant (aubergines) with salt and set aside for 30 minutes. Rinse under cold running water and pat dry with absorbent kitchen paper.

2 Heat oil in a heavy-based frying pan, add eggplant (aubergines) and cook, stirring frequently, for 5 minutes or until lightly browned. Remove eggplant (aubergines) from pan and set aside.

3 Add onion to pan and cook for 4-5 minutes or until soft. Stir in tomatoes, parsley, mint and reserved eggplant (aubergines) and cook, stirring frequently, for 5 minutes. Stir in rice and stock and bring to the boil. Reduce heat, cover and simmer for 30 minutes or until rice is tender. Allow to stand for 10 minutes before serving.

Serves 6

Pilau is a wonderful accompaniment that could easily be a meal on its own. This version with eggplant (aubergines) is particularly tasty and is great served with natural yogurt.

LONTONG

young banana leaves or aluminium foil
vegetable oil
500 g/1 lb short grain rice, washed
2 tablespoons soy sauce
2 tablespoons fried onion flakes

1 If using banana leaves, drop them into boiling water to clean and soften. Remove leaves from water and pat dry with absorbent kitchen paper. Cut leaves or foil into 20 cm/8 in squares and brush lightly with oil.

2 Place a large spoonful of rice in the centre of each square and fold over to completely encase rice and make a neat parcel. When making the parcels, allow a little room for expansion during cooking. Tie each parcel with string to secure.

3 Bring a large saucepan of water to the boil, drop in rice bundles and simmer for 1 hour. To serve, drain bundles, unwrap and sprinkle with soy sauce and onion flakes.

Serves 6

Lontong are traditionally wrapped in young banana leaves. If these are not readily available, you can successfully substitute aluminium foil. The fried onion flakes used in the recipe can be purchased from Asian food stores.

*Rose-scented Saffron Rice,
Pilau with Vegetables,
Lontong*

SIDE DISHES

RECIPE COLLECTION

PICKLED TOMATOES AND BEANS

This recipe uses canned three bean mix which is a mixture of butter beans, red kidney beans and lima beans. Any canned mixed beans can be used.

2 tablespoons olive oil
1 clove garlic, crushed
1 tablespoon chopped fresh basil
315 g/10 oz canned three bean mix, drained and rinsed
250 g/8 oz cherry tomatoes, halved
1 tablespoon white vinegar
1/2 teaspoon sugar

1 Heat oil in a large frying pan, add garlic and basil and cook for 1 minute. Stir in beans and tomatoes, cover and cook for 5-6 minutes.

2 Add vinegar and sugar and cook for 2 minutes longer or until heated through. Serve immediately.

Serves 4

CHILLI BEAN POTATOES

Oven temperature 220°C, 425 F, Gas 7

For a speedier version of this dish you can microwave the potatoes on HIGH (100%) for 10 minutes, or until tender, rather than baking them. Allow the potatoes to stand for at least 10 minutes before cutting and removing the flesh.

4 potatoes, scrubbed
1 tablespoon tomato paste (purée)
1-2 teaspoons chilli sauce, or according to taste
315 g/10 oz canned red kidney beans, drained and rinsed
freshly ground black pepper
paprika

1 Bake potatoes for 45-60 minutes or until soft. Remove from oven and allow to cool slightly.

2 Cut tops from potatoes, scoop out flesh, leaving a thin shell. Place potato flesh, tomato paste (purée) and chilli sauce in a bowl and mash. Stir in beans and season to taste with black pepper.

3 Spoon potato mixture into potato shells, dust with paprika and bake for 10-15 minutes or until heated through and lightly browned.

Serves 4

*Pickled Tomatoes and Beans,
Chilli Bean Potatoes*

SIDE DISHES

TECHNIQUES

INDIAN DHAL

250 g/8 oz brown or red lentils
4 cups/1 litre/1³/4 pt water
1 teaspoon ground turmeric
1 clove garlic, crushed
30 g/1 oz ghee or clarified butter
1 large onion, chopped
1 teaspoon garam masala
½ teaspoon ground ginger
1 teaspoon ground coriander
½ teaspoon cayenne pepper

3 Melt ghee or butter in a large frying pan, add onion and cook for 5 minutes or until onion is soft. Stir in garam masala, ginger, coriander and cayenne pepper and cook for 1 minute. Stir spice mixture into lentils and serve immediately.

1 Wash lentils in cold water.

2 Place lentils, water, turmeric and garlic in a large saucepan and bring to simmering. Cover and simmer, stirring occasionally, for 30 minutes or until lentils are cooked. Remove cover from pan, bring to the boil and boil to reduce excess liquid.

For a less fiery flavour, reduce the amount of cayenne pepper.

Serves 6

'Dhal is an Indian vegetarian dish made from lentils. In Hindustani the word for pulses (lentils, split peas and beans) is dhals. Yellow lentils are called toor dhal, pink lentils masoor dhal and yellow split peas channa dhal.'

Indian Dhal

RICE

TECHNIQUES

Hummus

Drizzling oil over the surface of the hummus prevents it from drying out.

---

125 g/4 oz chickpeas
4 cloves garlic, crushed
½ cup/125 g/4 oz tahini
4 tablespoons lemon juice
freshly ground black pepper
1 tablespoon olive oil
paprika

1 Place chickpeas in a large bowl, cover with water and set aside to soak overnight.

2 Drain chickpeas, place in a saucepan with enough water to cover and bring to the boil. Boil for 10 minutes then reduce heat and simmer for 1 hour or until tender. Drain and reserve a little of the cooking liquid. Place chickpeas and a little cooking liquid in a food processor or blender and process to form a smooth paste. Add garlic, tahini, lemon juice and black pepper to taste and process to combine.

Hummus is delicious served with pitta crisps or vegetable crudités. To make pitta crisps, split pitta bread and tear it into pieces. Place the pieces on a baking tray and cook at 150 C/300 F/Gas 2 for 10-15 minutes or until crisp.

---

3 Transfer hummus to a serving bowl, smooth surface, drizzle over oil and sprinkle with a little paprika.

Serves 12

PEARL BALLS

RICE

250 g/8 oz rice
15 g/½ oz dried mushrooms
boiling water
250 g/8 oz minced pork
4 spring onions, chopped
5 water chestnuts, sliced
1 teaspoon finely grated fresh ginger
1 clove garlic, crushed
2 tablespoons soy sauce
1 egg, lightly beaten

DIPPING SAUCE
½ cup/125 mL/4 fl oz soy sauce
½ teaspoon sesame oil
1 tablespoon chilli sauce, or according to taste

1 Place rice in a large bowl, cover with cold water and set aside to soak for 2 hours. Drain and spread out on absorbent kitchen paper to dry. Place mushrooms in a bowl, cover with boiling water and set aside to soak for 20 minutes or until mushrooms are tender. Drain, remove stalks if necessary and chop mushrooms.

2 Place mushrooms, pork, spring onions, water chestnuts, ginger, garlic, soy sauce and egg in a bowl and mix well to combine. Roll pork mixture into small balls, then roll in rice to coat. Place balls in a steamer, set over a saucepan of simmering water, cover and steam for 30 minutes or until rice swells and is cooked.

3 To make sauce, place soy sauce, oil and chilli sauce in a small bowl and mix to combine. Serve with Pearl Balls.

Makes 30

For a quicker version of this dish you can use precooked rice, in which case the soaking time of the rice is reduced to 10-15 minutes.

67

TECHNIQUES

Crunchy Split Peas

185 g/6 oz yellow split peas or 90 g/3 oz yellow split peas and 90 g/3 oz green split peas
2 teaspoons bicarbonate of soda
oil for deep-frying
½ teaspoon chilli powder
½ teaspoon ground coriander
pinch ground cinnamon
pinch ground cloves
1 teaspoon salt

1 Place split peas in a large bowl, cover with water, stir in bicarbonate of soda and set aside to soak overnight.

2 Rinse split peas under cold running water and drain thoroughly. Set aside for at least 30 minutes, then spread out on absorbent kitchen paper to dry. Heat about 5 cm/2 in oil in a frying pan and cook split peas in batches until golden. Using a slotted spoon, remove peas and drain on absorbent kitchen paper.

3 Transfer cooked peas to a dish, sprinkle with chilli powder, coriander, cinnamon, cloves and salt and toss to coat. Allow peas to cool and store in an airtight container.

Serves 8

Take care when frying the peas as even when completely dry they tend to cause the oil to bubble to the top of the pan.

'These spicy peas are delicious as a snack or pre-dinner nibble with drinks.'

Crunchy Split Peas

RICE

TECHNIQUES

SPICED CHICKEN PILAU

60 g/2 oz ghee or clarified butter
2 large onions, sliced
4 boneless chicken breast fillets, cubed
½ teaspoon ground turmeric
2 cups/440 g/14 oz basmati rice
4 cups/1 litre/1¾ pt boiling chicken stock
1 teaspoon cardamom seeds
½ teaspoon ground cinnamon
4 whole cloves
½ teaspoon ground fenugreek
125 g/4 oz fresh or frozen peas
90 g/3 oz unsalted cashew nuts
90 g/3 oz sultanas

1 Melt ghee or butter in a large saucepan, add onions and chicken and cook, stirring, for 3-4 minutes or until chicken changes colour. Stir in turmeric and rice and cook for 2 minutes longer. Add boiling stock, cardamom seeds, cinnamon, cloves and fenugreek and bring back to the boil. Stir well, reduce heat, cover and simmer for 20 minutes or until rice is cooked.

2 Add peas, cashew nuts and sultanas to rice mixture and fluff up with a fork, then cover and cook for 10 minutes longer. Fluff up again and serve immediately.

The traditional rice for an Indian pilau is basmati. Basmati rice is a long grain rice with a delicious nutlike flavour. If you do not have basmati rice any long grain rice can be used.

Serves 6

70

Falafel in Pitta Bread

4 large pitta bread rounds, warmed
shredded lettuce
onion slices
tomato slices

FALAFELS
440 g/14 oz canned chickpeas, drained
1 onion, quartered
2 cloves garlic, crushed
2 slices white bread
½ teaspoon cumin seeds
4 small dried chillies, seeded and crushed
1 tablespoon chopped fresh parsley
1 egg, lightly beaten
freshly ground black pepper
⅓ cup/45 g/1½ oz dried breadcrumbs
vegetable oil for deep-frying

1 To make Falafels, place chickpeas, onion, garlic, bread, cumin seeds and chillies in a food processor or blender and process until smooth. Transfer mixture to a bowl and stir in parsley, egg and black pepper to taste.

2 Divide mixture into eight equal portions and roll into balls. Roll balls in dried breadcrumbs, then flatten slightly to make an oval shape.

3 Heat oil in a deep saucepan until a cube of bread dropped in browns in 50 seconds. Cook Falafels a few at a time for 3 minutes or until golden. Remove and drain on absorbent kitchen paper.

4 Cut each pitta bread round in half and fill each half with a falafel, some lettuce and a few slices of onion and tomato. Serve immediately.

Makes 8

RICE

Do not add salt to the water when cooking legumes as this causes the skins to split and the insides to toughen.

All legumes should be brought to the boil and boiled rapidly for at least 5 minutes. Red kidney beans should be boiled for 10-15 minutes. The boiling kills toxins in the legumes.

TECHNIQUES

Vegetable Couscous

Originating from Morocco, couscous is often thought of as a type of grain; it is in fact a pasta made from durum wheat. However it is cooked and used in the same way as grains. The name refers to both the raw product and the cooked dish.

2 cups/250 g/8 oz couscous
2 cups/500 mL/16 fl oz water
4 tablespoons olive oil
2 onions, chopped
1 eggplant (aubergine), diced
500 g/1 lb pumpkin, acorn squash or marrow, diced
2 carrots, sliced
1 teaspoon chilli paste (sambal oelek)
2 tomatoes, peeled and chopped
2 tablespoons tomato purée
2 cups/500 mL/16 fl oz vegetable or chicken stock
440 g/14 oz canned chickpeas, drained
2 zucchini (courgettes), sliced
60 g/2 oz sultanas
2 tablespoons chopped fresh parsley

1 Place couscous and water in a large bowl and set aside to soak for 15 minutes or until water is absorbed. Heat oil in a large saucepan, add onions, eggplant (aubergine), pumpkin or squash and carrots and cook, stirring, for 5 minutes. Stir in chilli paste (sambal oelek), tomatoes, tomato purée and stock and bring to the boil.

2 Line a large metal sieve or colander with muslin or all-purpose kitchen cloth and place over saucepan. Place couscous in sieve or colander, then cover with aluminium foil and steam for 20 minutes. Remove sieve or colander and stir chickpeas, zucchini (courgettes) and sultanas into vegetable mixture. Replace sieve or colander, fluff up couscous with a fork, cover and steam for 20 minutes longer.

3 Spread couscous around the edge of a large serving dish. Stir parsley into vegetable mixture and spoon into the centre of the serving dish.

Serves 6

Greek Dolmades

RICE

185 g/6 oz packet vine leaves
2 tablespoons olive oil
1 onion, chopped
2 tablespoons chopped fresh mint
90 g/3 oz pine nuts, toasted
3/4 cup/170 g/5 1/2 oz rice, cooked
freshly ground black pepper

1 Drain vine leaves, rinse well and soak in cold water for 20 minutes. Carefully separate leaves and drain well.

2 Heat oil in a frying pan, add onion and cook for 5 minutes or until soft. Stir onion, mint and half the pine nuts into rice and season to taste with black pepper.

3 Place 2 teaspoons rice mixture on each vine leaf, fold in sides and roll up to form neat parcels.

4 Place dolmades side by side in a single layer in a shallow frying pan and pour over just enough hot water to cover. Place a plate on top of rolls, cover and simmer for 30 minutes. Remove pan from heat and set aside to cool, then remove dolmades to a plate, cover and refrigerate. Serve chilled, topped with remaining pine nuts.

Makes 45

Appearing throughout the cuisines of the Mediterranean it is the Greek *dolmades* and the Turkish *dolmas* that have found their way onto Western tables and are the most popular. Dolmades are usually filled with a seasoned rice mixture, while dolmas can also include meat or chicken.

INGREDIENTS

Cooking Rice and Legumes

You win two ways when you cook with rice and beans: firstly in your wallet, as these dietary staples are remarkably economical; secondly in your health, as there are few foods more nutritious.

TIPS FOR COOKING LEGUMES

All legumes except lentils and split peas require soaking before cooking. Soaking helps to clean and soften them.

- Soaking lentils and split peas will speed up the cooking time. Depending on how much time is available, legumes can either have a long or a short soak.

- Do not add salt to the cooking water as this causes the skins to split and the insides to toughen.

- The cooking time depends on the type, age and quality of the beans. The fresher the beans, the shorter the cooking time.

- All legumes should be brought to the boil and boiled rapidly for at least 5 minutes.

- Red kidney beans should be boiled for 10-15 minutes to kill the toxins in them.

- Always cook legumes in a large saucepan with enough cold water to cover them by 5 cm/2 in.

LONG SOAK

This method of preparation requires a little forethought. To prepare legumes, rinse, then place them in a large bowl. Cover with cold water, then cover the bowl and set aside to soak overnight at room temperature. If soaking lentils or split peas, only 10 minutes is required. Drain and replace the water before cooking.

SHORT SOAK

For this method simply place the legumes in a large saucepan, cover them with water and bring to the boil. Reduce the heat and simmer for 5 minutes. Remove the pan from the heat and set aside to soak for 1-2 hours (see Legume Cooking Chart for the time required). Drain and rinse before using.

It is the *dried* seeds or beans of the plants from the *Leguminosae* family that are referred to as legumes or pulses; namely dried peas, beans and lentils.

LEGUME COOKING CHART

Legume	Short Soak Time	Cooking Time
Adzuki beans	1 hour	30-45 minutes
Black-eyed beans	1 hour	45-60 minutes
Borlotti beans	1 hour	$1\frac{1}{4}$-$1\frac{1}{2}$ hours
Butter or lima beans	1 hour	1-$1\frac{1}{2}$ hours
Cannellini beans	1 hour	1-$1\frac{1}{2}$ hours
Chickpeas	2 hours	1-$1\frac{1}{2}$ hours
Haricot beans	1 hour	1 hour
Lentils	—	30 minutes
Pinto beans	1 hour	$1\frac{1}{4}$ hours
Red kidney beans	1 hour	$1\frac{1}{4}$-$1\frac{1}{2}$ hours
Soya beans	2 hours	2-4 hours
Split peas	—	30 minutes

RICE

From left: Yellow lentils, adzuki beans, haricot beans, green split peas, red kidney beans, brown lentils, cannellini beans

INGREDIENTS

A Guide to Rice and Legumes

RICE

At least one-third of the human race eats rice as a staple food. There are many varieties and no preparation is required. Cooking varies according to the type of rice and the recipe.

Short grain rice: The most popular all-purpose rice, particularly suited to dishes where grains need to cling together.

Long grain rice: Known for its fluffy texture, long grain rice is good for pilaus, salads and stuffings.

Brown rice: Natural unpolished rice that has a distinctive nutty taste.

Basmati rice: Grown in Bangladesh and Pakistan, this rice is a delicious aromatic rice ideal for highly spiced Indian dishes.

Arborio or risotto rice: An Italian rice that is ideal for absorbing a great deal of liquid. Generally used for risotto and jambalaya.

Wild rice: Although related to the rice family, wild rice is actually a seed from an aquatic grass which grows in North America. It has an appealing distinctive nutty flavour. It is quite expensive, and is used more commonly in gourmet cooking.

LEGUMES

Adzuki beans: Small reddish-brown beans with a cream-coloured seam. Their creamy texture is particularly popular in Japan and China where they are used boiled, mashed and sweetened in cakes and desserts. They can also be used in soups, pâtés and savoury dishes.

Black beans: Small, almost round, black beans with a white seam. Popular in the West Indies and in Chinese cuisine. They are a sweet-tasting bean that can be used in soups, salads and savoury dishes.

Broad beans: Flat beans native to North Africa ranging in colour from olive green to brown cream. Initially cultivated by the ancient Egyptians and Greeks. They are known in Europe as Fava beans and are mostly eaten dried. Broad beans are also eaten fresh.

Butter beans: Native to South America, these large plump, white beans are similar in shape to broad beans. Available fresh, dried, canned and frozen.

Cannellini beans: White kidney beans with square ends. Popular in Italian cuisine. Delicious in soups and salads or in place of haricot beans to make baked beans.

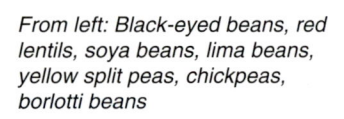

From left: Black-eyed beans, red lentils, soya beans, lima beans, yellow split peas, chickpeas, borlotti beans

RICE

Chickpeas: Available as white garbanzo or small, brown desi chickpeas. Both are round and rough textured with a pointed beard at one end. They are crunchy with a nutty flavour and are popular in Middle Eastern cooking where they are combined with tahini, lemon and garlic to make hummus. In Israel they are used to make a version of falafel. In Greece, roasted chickpeas are served with drinks.

Haricot/Navy beans: Small white oval beans. The term haricot derives from medieval times when dried beans were used chiefly in a pot containing a haricot of meat. Probably best known for their use in commercial baked beans, they were commonly served to the US Navy, hence the alternative name. These beans are also delicious in casseroles.

Lentils: Popular in European and Indian cuisine, lentils are available in brown, green, orange, yellow and black. They are lens-shaped and may be bought whole or split. Used in soups and casseroles, they are also the main ingredient of the well-known Indian dip, dhal.

Lima beans: Native to South America, lima beans are flat kidney-shaped beans which can be either small and green or large and white. They have a soft floury texture and are popular in both salads and hot dishes.

Mung beans: Widely cultivated in India and China, these small olive green beans are available whole, split and skinless. They are commonly used in stews and salads but are best known in their sprouted form as bean sprouts.

Red kidney beans: Sweet-tasting, red, kidney-shaped beans. They are mostly used in soups, stews and salads, and traditionally used in Creole cooking and in the Mexican dish chilli con carne.

Soya beans: These small, hard, oval, beige beans are extremely versatile. Originally cultivated in China, soya beans are possibly the most nutritious of all beans and are best known for their by-products, which include soy sauce, tofu (bean curd), miso (fermented soya beans) and tempeh (fermented bean paste). Soya beans are also used to make textured vegetable protein (TVP) and soy bean milk.

Split peas: Green and yellow peas are available. The green pea is traditionally used in the English pease pudding. The yellow variety is puréed for soup. In Sweden, this soup is traditionally served on a Thursday evening, to commemorate the day of the last supper of the unpopular King Eric XIV, who was poisoned by a dash of arsenic in his split pea soup!

INGREDIENTS

RICE COOKING CHART

Method	White Rice	Brown Rice
Rapid boil	Place 8 cups/2 litres/3$\frac{1}{2}$ pt water in a large saucepan and bring to the boil. Stir in 1 cup/220 g/7 oz rice and return to the boil. Boil rapidly for 12-15 minutes or until rice is tender. Drain through a sieve or colander and serve.	Place 8 cups/2 litres/3$\frac{1}{2}$ pt water in a large saucepan and bring to the boil. Stir in 1 cup/220 g/7 oz rice and return to the boil. Boil rapidly for 30-40 minutes or until rice is tender. Drain and serve.
Absorption An easy way to cook rice, and the grains stay separate and fluffy.	Place 1$\frac{1}{2}$ cups/375 mL/12 fl oz water in a large saucepan, stir in 1 cup/220 g/7 oz rice. Cover and simmer for 20-25 minutes. Uncover, toss with a fork and stand for a few minutes before serving.	Place 2 cups/500 mL/16 fl oz water in a large saucepan and bring to the boil. Stir in 1 cup/220 g/7 oz rice, cover and simmer for 55 minutes or until all the liquid is absorbed. Toss with a fork and serve.
Steaming This is a popular Chinese method of cooking rice.	Wash 1 cup/220 g/7 oz rice, then drain and set aside to dry. Place rice in a heavy-based saucepan and add enough water to cover the rice by 2.5 cm/1 in. Bring to the boil and boil rapidly until steam holes appear on the surface of the rice. Reduce heat to as low as possible, cover with a tight-fitting lid, or foil, and steam for 10 minutes. Remove lid, or foil, toss with a fork and stand 5 minutes before serving.	Wash 1 cup/220 g/7 oz rice, then drain and set aside to dry. Place rice in a heavy-based saucepan and add enough water to cover the rice by 2.5 cm/1 in. Bring to the boil and boil rapidly until steam holes appear on the surface of the rice. Reduce heat to as low as possible, cover with a tight-fitting lid, or foil, and steam for 25-30 minutes. Remove lid or foil, toss with a fork and stand 5 minutes before serving.
Microwave Cooking rice in the microwave does not save time but it does guarantee a perfect result and there is no messy saucepan at the end of the cooking time.	Place 1 cup/220 g/7 oz rice and 2 cups/500 mL/16 fl oz water in a large microwave-safe container. Cook, uncovered, on HIGH (100%) for 12-15 minutes or until liquid is absorbed. Cover and stand for 5 minutes. Toss with a fork and serve.	Place 1 cup/220 g/7 oz rice and 3 cups/750 mL/1$\frac{1}{4}$ pt water in a large microwave-safe container. Cook, uncovered, on HIGH (100%) for 30-35 minutes or until liquid is absorbed. Stir occasionally during cooking. Cover and stand for 5 minutes. Toss with a fork and serve.

INDEX

Artichoke
    and Bean Salad 56
    Risotto 39
Asparagus and Bacon Risotto 42
Avocado Sauce 47
Baked Cheese Custard 13
Barley
    Casserole 21
    Golden Grain Salad 56
    and Mushroom Soup 4
Basmati Rice
    Rose-scented Saffron 59
    Spiced Broccoli Pilau 59
    Spiced Chicken Pilau 70
Beans
    see also Haricot Beans; Red
        Kidney Beans
    and Artichoke Salad 56
    and Bacon Salad 55
    Black Bean Hotpot 20
    Cottage Pie 29
    Hotpot 16
    Mung Bean Frittata 34
    Patties with Avocado Sauce 47
    and Tomatoes, Pickled 62
    Vegetable Chilli 25
    and Vegetable Risotto 43
Beef and Brown Rice Pie 12
Black Bean Hotpot 20
Broccoli
    and Rice Soufflé 32
    Spiced Pilau 59
Brown Rice
    and Beef Pie 12
    and Cheese Pie 46
    Fritters 34
    Golden Grain Salad 56
    Paella 15
    Stuffing 22
    and Vegetable Patties 30
Burgers, Lentil 33
Cabbage Rolls 11
Cheese
    Baked Custard 13
    and Brown Rice Pie 46
    and Rice-filled Eggplant 14
    Rice with Herbs 26

Risotto 42
Chicken
    Poussin with Rice Stuffing 22
    Spiced Pilau 70
Chickpeas
    Falafel in Pitta Bread 71
    Fritters 18
    Hummus 66
Chilli
    Bean Potatoes 62
    Rice Balls 3
Coconut Cream 34
Coriander Sauce 6
Couscous
    Golden Grain Salad 56
    Vegetable 72
Crunchy Split Peas 68
Curry, Vegetable and Lentil 48
Custard, Baked Cheese 13
Dhal, Indian 64
Dip 67
    Red Bean 9
Dolmades 6
    Greek 73
Dressing
    French 55
    Garlic 51
    Kiwi Fruit 29
    Orange 56
    Spicy 45
Eggplant, Rice-filled 14
Falafel in Pitta Bread 71
French Dressing 55
Frittata, Mung Bean 34
Fritters
    Chickpea 18
    Rice 34
Garbanzo Beans see Chickpeas
Garlic Dressing 51
Golden Grain Salad 56
Greek Dolmades 73
Haricot Beans
    Soup 8
    Tuna Salad 54
Hummus 66
Indian Dhal 64
Kiwi Fruit Dressing 29
Leek Sauce 5
Lentil
    Burgers 33
    Indian Dhal 64
    Pockets 37

and Rice Dolmades 6
    Salad 45
    Spicy Vegetable Loaf 48
    and Vegetable Curry 48
    Wontons 6
Lontong 60
Mung Bean Frittata 34
Mushroom
    and Barley Soup 4
    Risotto 39
Orange Dressing 56
Paella 15
    Salad 51
Pearl Balls 67
Peppers, Sausage-filled 17
Pickled Tomatoes and Beans 62
Pie
    Bean Cottage 29
    Brown Rice and Beef 12
    Cheesy Brown Rice 46
    Vegetable and Rice 24
Pilau
    Spiced Broccoli 59
    Spiced Chicken 70
    with Vegetables 60
Polenta and Salami Bake 26
Pork Pearl Balls 67
Potatoes, Chilli Bean 62
Poussin with Rice Stuffing 22
Prawn Risotto 40
Pumpkins with Bean Filling 30
Rainbow Risotto 22
Red Hot Beans 45
Red Kidney Beans
    Chilli Potatoes 62
    Dip 9
    Filled Pumpkins 30
    Filled Tacos 36
    Red Hot 45
    Sausage-filled Peppers 17
Rice
    see also Basmati Rice; Brown Rice;
        Risotto
    Baked Cheese Custard 13
    and Broccoli Soufflé 32
    Cabbage Rolls 11
    with Cheese and Herbs 26
    Chilli Balls 3
    Filled Eggplant 14
    Filled Tomatoes 5
    Greek Dolmades 73

and Lentil Dolmades 6
Lontong 60
Pearl Balls 67
Pilau with Vegetables 60
Salmon Loaf 11
Terrine 19
and Vegetable Pie 24
Wild Rice Salad 29
Risotto
    Artichoke 39
    with Asparagus and Bacon 42
    with Cheese 42
    Creamy Mushroom 39
    Moulded Tomato 41
    Prawn 40
    Rainbow 22
    with Spinach and Herbs 42
    Vegetable and Bean 43
Rose-scented Saffron Rice 59
Saffron Rice, Rose-scented 59
Salad
    Bean and Artichoke 56
    Bean and Bacon 55
    Golden Grain 56
    Lentil 45

Seafood Paella 51
Tuna and Bean 54
Wild Rice 29
Salmon Rice Loaf 11
Sauce
    Avocado 47
    Coriander 6
    Creamy Leek 5
    Dipping 67
    White 26
    Yogurt 18
    Yogurt Mint 33
Sausage-filled Peppers 17
Seafood Paella Salad 51
Soufflé, Broccoli and Rice 32
Soup
    Hearty Bean 8
    Mushroom and Barley 4
Spiced Broccoli Pilau 59
Spiced Chicken Pilau 70
Spinach and Herb Risotto 42
Split Peas, Crunchy 68
Tacos, Bean-filled 36
Terrine, Rice 19
Tomatoes

and Beans, Pickled 62
Rice-filled 5
Risotto 41
Tuna Bean Salad 54
Vegetable
    and Bean Risotto 43
    Chilli 25
    Couscous 72
    and Lentil Curry 48
    Spicy Loaf 48
    Pilau 60
    and Rice Patties 30
    and Rice Pie 24
White Sauce 26
Wild Rice Salad 29
Wontons, Lentil 6
Yogurt
    Mint Sauce 33
    Sauce 18

UK COOKERY EDITOR
Katie Swallow

EDITORIAL
Food Editor: Rachel Blackmore
Editorial Assistant: Ella Martin
Editorial Coordinator: Margaret Kelly
Recipe Development: Sheryle Eastwood, Lucy Kelly, Donna Hay,
Anneka Mitchell, Penelope Peel, Belinda Warn, Loukie Werle
Credits: Recipes pages 9, 64, 70, 71, 72 by Louise Steel; pages 66, 68, 73
by June Budgen; page 67 by Annette Grimsdale © Merehurst Limited

COVER
Photography: Ashley Mackevicius
Styling: Wendy Berecry
Plate from Villeroy and Boch

PHOTOGRAPHY
Per Ericson, Paul Grater, Ray Joyce, Ashley Mackevicius, Harm Mol,
Yanto Noerianto, Andy Payne, Warren Webb

STYLING
Wendy Berecry, Belinda Clayton, Rosemary De Santis, Carolyn
Fienberg, Jacqui Hing, Michelle Gorry

DESIGN AND PRODUCTION
Manager: Sheridan Carter
Layout: Lulu Dougherty
Finished Art: Stephen Joseph
Design: Frank Pithers

Published by J.B. Fairfax Press Pty Ltd
A.C.N. 003 738 430
Formatted by J.B. Fairfax Press Pty Ltd
Output by Adtype, Sydney
Printed by Toppan Printing Co, Hong Kong

© J.B. Fairfax Press Pty Ltd, 1992
This book is copyright. No part may be reproduced or transmitted
without the written permission of the publisher. Enquiries should be
made in writing to the publisher.
Includes Index
1 86343 096 2 (pbk)
1 85391 293 X

Distributed by J.B. Fairfax Press Ltd
9 Trinity Centre, Park Farm Estate
Wellingborough, Northants
Ph: (0933) 402330 Fax: (0933) 402234